POWER AND PROTOCOL

FOR GETTING

TO THE TOP

The Image, the Moves, the Smarts

for Business and Social Success

OTHER BOOKS
BY JEFFREY P. DAVIDSON

POWER AND PROTOCOL
FOR GETTING
TO THE TOP

The Image, the Moves, the Smarts
for Business and Social Success

Jeffrey P. Davidson,
M.B.A, C.M.C.

SHAPOLSKY PUBLISHERS, INC.
NEW YORK

A Shapolsky Book

For any additional information, contact:
Shapolsky Publishers, Inc.
136 West 22nd Street
New York NY 10011
(212) 633-2022

10 9 8 7 6 5 4 3 2

Library of Congress Cataloging-in-Publication Data

Davidson, Jeffrey P., 19-
    Power and protocol for getting to the top: the image, the moves. the smarts for business and social success / Jeffrey P. Davidson.
    p.   cm.
    Includes bibliographical references and index.
    ISBN 0-944007-68-6
    1. Business etiquette. 2. Executives. I. Title.
HF5389.D28   1991
395'.52—dc20   90-20095

Design and Typography by Sally Ann Zegarelli
Long Branch, NJ 07740

Printed and bound by Graficromo s.a., Cordoba, Spain

This book is dedicated to people who do hard work but never get the credit, appreciation, or compensation they deserve. It's dedicated to teachers and nurses, police officers and fire fighters, mothers and fathers, and all others who constitute the fabric of our society. And it's also dedicated to Valerie Anne, 68 days old, and roarin' to go!

ACKNOWLEDGMENTS

In alphabetical order, I wish to thank Don Bagin, Ph.D.; Letitia Baldrige; Susan K. Barnes; Mylle Bell; Don Beveridge, Jr.; Jonathan Blum; Ron Brady; Dan Burrus; Maryles Casto; Robert Cialdini, Ph.D.; Herb Cohen; Sherrie Connelly, Ph.D.; Nancy Davidson, Ph.D.; Susan Davidson; Stanley Davis, Ph.D.; Roger Dawson; Janet G. Elsea, Ph.D.; Sybil Ferguson; Roger Fisher, Ph.D.; as well as Charles Garfield, Ph.D.; Charles Givens; and Carole Jackson.

Continuing alphabetically, thanks go to Elizabeth Jeffries; Karen Kalish; Chester Karrass, Ph.D.; Richard Levy; Judith Martin; Mark McCormack; Judith Monson; Edward Mrkvicka, Jr.; Gerald Nierenberg, Ph.D.; David Ogilvy; Warren Pelton, Ph.D.; Dr. Norman Vincent Peale; Neil Rackham; Susan RoAne; Anthony Robbins; Raphael Sagalyn; Richard Staron; W. Clement Stone; Joseph Sugarman; Gerry Tausch; Juanell Teague; and William Ury, Ph.D.—for their thoughts, words, examples, conduct, or subject matter expertise.

Thanks, too, to Edie Fraser, Willis Shen, Robert Smith-Midford, Katherine J. Reynolds, and Dianne Walbrecker for their research and editorial assistance, and to Judy Dubler for word processing.

Finally, thanks are due to Ian Shapolsky for spearheading the project and generating considerable interest, Donn Teal for a fine editing job, Annie Cohen for marketing it, Brian

Feinblum in publicity, and all the other fine folks at Shapolsky Publishers; and to Robert Salomon and Gary Fitzgerald of the Carol Publishing Group for their substantial, ongoing efforts.

Jeffrey P. Davidson
Falls Church, Virginia
1991

CONTENTS

INTRODUCTION

Getting to the top and staying there—that's the goal of aspiring executives, entrepreneurs, and career professionals. To break into the winner's circle requires insider information: knowing what the people at the top know that you don't know. This book provides a wide-angle view of effective strategies for your business and social success.

Power and Protocol for Getting to the Top is an insider's look at how successful, rich, and powerful people in our society project the right image and make the right moves to climb to the peak in their fields—and enjoy the view.

This book will show you hundreds of potent approaches to getting to the top—time-tested advice that has worked for the people at the top in business and in other fields. Minimizing discussion of widely covered topics such as networking and mentoring, the book refreshingly illuminates the essence of what it really takes to flourish in business in the 1990s.

Power and Protocol for Getting to the Top draws upon first-person observation and careful research. It reflects the experiences of both contemporary business individuals and historical figures. Some of the topics covered include:

- why it's what you know, and how you use it, that counts
- how to "up" your achievement potential
- protocol for social and business functions
- appropriate gift-giving
- greeting and meeting others for lasting impact

- reading and leading people
- winning strategies for negotiations
- projecting the right image
- corporate and entrepreneurial women at the top
- keeping pace with change

I hope you finish this book feeling supercharged and powerfully focused on *your* journey to the top.

PART I

AT THE TOP

Chapter One

DO THE RIGHT THING

Personally I am always ready to learn, although I do not like being taught.

—Winston Churchill

Some call it protocol. Others just call it expected behavior. It boils down to doing things right *and* doing the right things. Successful people—those who have achieved the top-rung status of wealth, fame and/or position—seem to know something special about the right moves in business and social situations and how to consistently make them. They pretty much always look right, say the right things, go to the right places, arrive at the right time and associate with the right people. They tend not to put their feet in their mouths, and rarely slip up, at least when in public.

People at the top seem to be born knowing just what to do in nearly every situation and exactly how to do it. Although there are many "how-to" success guides and books on business etiquette, they can't cover every possible situation; yet those at the top seem uncannily adept at ad-libbing their way to success. If this ability is in the genes or taught early in life,

3

how do we explain the poor boy or girl made-good who seems to so readily take on the trappings of power and does things just right?

Are they self-taught or did someone coach them?

The plausible answer is that they watched and studied, beginning well ahead of the time that they reached the top. In fact, their ability *to catch on to the proper behavior at the top helped them get to the top.*

People who are able to act successful have a much better chance of eventually being successful.

What these people know and do differently is the focus of this book. We'll explore some key observations about what the successful/powerful/wealthy know and do in the areas of

- achievement
- leadership
- negotiating, and
- projecting an appropriate image

We'll also explore related issues such as how the people at the top handle their wealth, and the special challenges for women at the top.

In this chapter we'll cover social and business protocol in general. What the people at the top (PATTs) know is usually quite subtle and often subconscious. It's as if they are following the rules of a special game that were passed on to them in unspoken ways because these rules don't appear in books. In fact, the unavailability of information on this subject is one of the primary reason why I decided to write *Power and Protocol for Getting to the Top.*

A MATTER OF DEGREE

Much of what is done correctly by those who have risen to the top relates to appearance and manner, how to look and how to act. Much of the "right way" they look and act is related to a matter of degree; neither too much nor too little. Understatement in mannerisms, speech and appearance is the key. After all, these are people who are noticed for their correctness, not for their flamboyance.

To state the obvious, the man on the way up will always choose a pair of classic designer loafers or a Chanel suit over cowboy boots (even at the height of yet another predictable comeback for all things Western). The woman on the way up will always wear a classic designer outfit over a loud-colored miniskirt. Any suggestion of extremes or notoriety is considered too "nouveau" and smacks of a "Look, Ma, I finally made it to the top!" mentality. The dark green Mercedes is selected over the white stretch limo. The voice is modulated to a quiet monotone that causes everyone else to lean forward and listen.

While successful people are visible people, they usually are careful to not be "overexposed." They show up at enough social and political events, gallery openings and charity balls to keep in circulation, but they don't make the rounds of "in" places too frequently. In their business dealings, they are equally conscious of the right degree of visibility. It is not necessary to attend every meeting or every conference. They can pick and choose, sending underlings to attend functions that may be slightly less essential.

Confidence in Your Staff

Each year, the American Bookseller Association holds its annual convention in a major U.S. city. Richard Staron, publisher of BusinessOne–Irwin (formerly Dow Jones–Irwin) has a vested interest in the success of his publishing house at this annual event. In 1987, when the ABA convention was held in New Orleans, Staron declined to attend. When asked why, he said he didn't like New Orleans and preferred not to travel there.

Staron wasn't being capricious; he simply knew where and when he worked best and avoided what didn't fit for him. Also, with Staron's careful selection of staff he felt at ease in letting them run the show without him in New Orleans.

KNOWLEDGE PUT TO GOOD USE

A good portion of the "correctness" exercised by those at the top derives from their desire to be sure they are behaving appropriately at all times. These individuals really do work at maintaining protocol. For example, when determining who sits next to whom at dinner parties that include two foreign ambassadors and a retired admiral, or two Chief Executive Officers and the Undersecretary at the Department of Commerce, there is no substitute for using good sense and good taste in making the seating arrangements. They make it their business to learn about everything from what to wear to a best friend's third wedding, to how much time should pass between the dinner and a not-too-early departure from a party.

They know that *knowledge of proper protocol is not only power, it is the clearest evidence of being powerful.*

People who are at the top often have a knack for keeping up with what is going on, and they find many ways to use that knowledge every day; in conversation and in decision making.

> They make it their business to be informed about what is taking place around them, from who just acquired a house in the country, to who is having a baby, to who just got a promotion.
>
> They also take the trouble to find out the names of an important business client's secretary, wife, or husband.

Predictably, people at the top (PATTs) then use what they know in conversation and when taking action. They are often well read and exceedingly thoughtful. Not uncommon is this type of business greeting: "Hello, Harold [a client]. Glad I caught you. Barbara [the client's secretary] said you might be in that meeting all day. Oh, before I forget, when does Elena [the client's wife] get home from the hospital?" This concern reflects propriety and politeness while also conveying a subtle form of one-upmanship. Power between two people, in its simplest form, is held by the person *who knows the most about the other*.

USE OF SYMBOLS

The appearance of being successful often is a key element in actually becoming and remaining successful (explored in greater detail in Chapter 6). Other things being equal, the more one appears headed for the top, the greater the chances he/she will reach that lofty pinnacle. PATTs know that symbols do count, but not when they're flaunted. It's another matter of degree.

If the symbol is overused, such as the distinct yellow power tie or the car phone, it may detract from one's overall power image, unless the symbol itself has become a "classic," like a pair of Barcelona chairs in the office, a Jaguar in the garage and/or engraved business cards in the wallet.

PATTs, much like others, find it difficult to keep up with what is "in" and "out" in terms of power symbols. Just as something becomes "in" for the uppermost echelons, its price often drops and it is adopted by mid-level executives and then it usually trickles down to entry-level executives. Speaker phones and then car phones were once power toys, however brief their reign. Cellular phones carried in brief cases will probably soon bite the dust also.

Perhaps nothing has endured as many styles and fads as that ever-present power symbol, the briefcase. Big was in for awhile; then small. The briefcase, as a symbol, is something that those at the very top don't worry about much; when they go to a meeting, someone else is carrying all the necessary documents.

When things get too trendy or faddish, PATTs often respond by returning to tradition. For example, instead of taking their paging beeper or a cellular phone to a restaurant, they now often ask the maître d' to bring a restaurant phone to their table—just like business executives and the well-to-do did 20 years ago.

Signature Symbols

PATTs invest in and cultivate "signature symbols." These are items that are distinctively their own, so much so that no acquaintance would dare adopt them. Special cufflinks and black buckles or a rare desk set qualify here. A constant supply of gardenias, arranged in Steuben bowls in the office and at home also creates a signature symbol.

Likewise, an unusual French wine, always cooling in a nearby refrigerator, is also a signature symbol. Colors or color combinations (if not too trendy), distinct genres of art, or fine old fountain pens have all been used as signature symbols.

The key to their effective use is frequency of display. PATTs know not to overexpose the use of these symbols, but to make them just evident enough to become representative.

POISE AND EXECUTION

PATTs can adapt their style depending on the degree of formality, the level of seriousness and the people involved. They have in the back of their minds a subconscious idea of their desired outcomes. These might range from negotiating a future business deal to hosting a successful dinner party.

They have an innate, if not learned, sense of poise for most occasions, from business meetings to cocktail parties and from extending thanks to asking for charitable contributions. They master the "what-to-do" (the protocol of the situation) and "how-to-do-it" (the think-on-your-feet part).

Arsenio Hall

When the earthquake struck in California on October 18, 1989, Arsenio Hall was in the middle of taping his TV talk show for that evening. Informed of the quake during a commercial, while interviewing a guest, Hall strategically decided to ignore mentioning the quake. The show would conclude in another 20 minutes and there was no apparent need to alarm anyone in the audience.

Hall didn't have details as to the extent of the quake and damage, and since the show would be aired that night he felt there was no point in making any statement that later would prove to be inaccurate or inappropriate. In an era where many media hosts covet being the first to deliver late-breaking news, Hall decided to remain steadfast on another course—to host the best show that he could, and leave news coverage to those more qualified to do so.

The ability to rise to handle a wide variety of situations with composure and to project unquestionable success is an art, but it is only one of many skills which readily distinguish the people at the top of their professions.

THE ART OF THE INTRODUCTION

The mechanics of the greeting or introduction at the start of business or social conversations are a matter of convention, and PATTs must know who should speak first, whose name should be used first, and so on.

> Greetings and introductions should begin with people of the highest corporate rank and work downward until everyone in the room is introduced.
>
> It is important to state each person's name and position or rank in the firm when making introductions, and to go slowly enough so that everyone clearly hears the name of everyone else.

While it might seem that a different or more casual approach would be more distinctive, it's not good form to stray from the norm during formal occasions. Such was the case of a U.S. senator who was on a Senate Committee that had a meeting with Jordan's King Hussein.

The particular senator, who prided himself on his "country casual" demeanor, missed the protocol officer's briefing before the king arrived. He entered the committee room after the king had already been greeted by the others with the proper, "How do you do, Your Highness" (*not* "King Hussein" and not "Your Royal Highness"). The senator simply strode over to the king, patted him on the back and grinned, "Hi ya, King." Distinctive, but certainly not classy, and not likely to earn the respect of the king or anyone else in attendance.

Likewise, following their Superbowl-winning season in 1988, Washington Redskins hero John Riggins was at a black tie dinner where he told Supreme Court Justice Sandra Day O'Connor to "loosen up Sandy, baby," just before he passed out drunk. The incident contributed nicely to the already steep

Riggins lore, but probably hasn't done much to help his post-football career.

Using People's Names

PATTs know the importance of using a person's name. Our name's are the "sweetest and most important sound in the English language" to many of us. The accurate use of names is crucial in greetings, and PATTs are especially adept at remembering and using names. Some naturally have good memories; many others take memory enhancement courses to learn and practice the many tricks for remembering. They know how important this social grace really can be. To address someone you have recently met with confidence and without mixing up his name is to open the door of opportunity.

When a PATT meets someone for the second time, and the first was months earlier, he should be able to say with ease, "Well hello, Lynn. It's good to see you again." This doesn't always stem from a strong memory, however. Often it means that the greeter pulled his/her host aside just minutes before to refresh his memory about the person's name. PATTs know it is important for people to think they have made enough of a positive impression so that their name will be remembered.

Politicians rely on their handlers to give them instant name recollection. Often, when an aid leans over to say something to the politician, that something is the name and a quick description of someone whom the PATT should know by name and by accomplishment.

One chief executive officer of a large electronics company has trained his secretary to make calls before a meeting or social event and create a list of the names of people who will be there. He studies the list on the way to the event, putting faces with names in his mind so he wouldn't be surprised by someone whose name he couldn't remember. Other PATTs grill their spouses before hand to pool information that allows

11

both of them to shine in terms of name recognition and comfortable greetings.

Nevertheless, PATTs suffer memory lapses just like everyone else. When this happens, the successful people know that faking familiarity is the worst response. "Well, hi there, how are you?" is not good tact when you can't remember anything about a person, other than a vague sense that you've seen him or her before. Inevitably, that starts a fairly affable conversation. And then, the worst scenario happens: a third person enters the scene who you should introduce to X; but since you don't know X's real name, you've just dug yourself an even deeper hole.

The easiest memory lapse to handle is one that occurs rather instantly, within only a short period after being introduced to someone for the first time.

The appropriate response in this case becomes: "I'm sorry, I didn't catch your name."

For those lapses that occur much later, people who deal with the unfortunate situation best deal with it soonest.

The typical conversation goes: "Well, hi, Mary. Where have you been hiding?" Response of Mary (a PATT): "It's good to see you again. I'm *so* sorry, but I have just drawn a blank on your name." "John Smith." "Of course, John. I can't believe I did that."

Saying the name aloud as soon as possible helps recapture some warmth and make up for the embarrassing memory lapse.

Successful people generally have a lot of little ways of putting those around them at ease. For instance, they are savvy enough to anticipate when someone is likely to forget their name. They just seem to know when someone they are meeting for a second time has forgotten their name, and immediately supplement their initial greeting with something like, "I don't know if you remember me, Ed Jackson. We met . . ."

Handshakes and Hugs

PATTs regard the handshake as a key factor in the greeting, as well as in departures and when closing business deals. Many even practice to get it right. A bank president describes the ideal grip as, "Firm, but not tugging. Two pumps maximum." He mentions that every so often he practices his handshake on himself, gripping his left hand with his right to make sure he's using just the right amount of pressure.

"I'm very conscious of not letting my handshake go dead fish, but sometimes I have a problem with cold hands." The solution: at parties he is careful to always hold his cold drink in his left hand and to stretch and contract the fingers of his right hand as much as possible. As a rule, PATTs are never bonecrushers. The bonecrusher, and we've all met them, impresses no one, and has left many walking away in disbelief after the inappropriate handshake, not to mention their injured hands.

Although social hugs and kisses are said to have started with the upper crust of society, those at the top are turning their collective backs on the phenomenon. "It has gotten too confusing to know who and when to kiss," says one top executive. "So, I decided to eliminate it entirely and go solely with hand shakes."

Judith Martin, author of the syndicated *Miss Manners* column, says, "Kissing has gotten completely out of hand, and no one can agree on the system." The confusion includes questions about whether two women should kiss, or just members of the opposite sex, and about what occasions (i.e., business as well as social) are appropriate for kissing.

When someone does start hugging or kissing, it is best to not embarrass this person and go with the flow. One top executive who says he has given up on hugging and kissing greetings keeps a special handshake in reserve. This "covered handshake" involves shaking a little longer, right hand-to-right hand, while putting his left hand over the clasped right hands. This additional touching gesture is often used for occasions that warrant a little more warmth and closeness.

Exhibiting Host Behavior

At a Chamber of Commerce reception in an upscale hotel, small pockets of people congregate between the bar at one end of the room and the table full of hors d'oeuvres at the other end. The dress is formal, the mood festive, and the opportunity for making new business contacts, even on this social level, are ripe.

If you stand on a balcony overlooking the scene, several types of behavior become quite clear. There are stragglers, not acquainted with any one, who stick close to the food or drink. Likewise, there are small cliques of people who know each other, work with each other on committees and feel safe by forming tight social circles and speaking only among themselves.

If you watch closely, however, you will spot at least one person, smiling and gracious, moving around the room fluidly, shaking hands and introducing himself or herself with direct eye contact and a warm smile. Unlike the quick hitters, however, this person spends time with each individual he or she greets, listening carefully while the other talks. This person's interest and energy in meeting new people is obvious.

Is this person the president of the Chamber or Commerce, someone whose responsibility it is to act as host? Perhaps. Just as likely that person is a new member or a guest. Whatever his current status in the group, you can be sure he is successful. He understands a critical factor in human relations, described eloquently by Susan RoAne in her book *How to Work a Room*, and before her by Dr. Adele Scheele in *Skills for Success* —the importance of acting as a host.

PATTs don't wait for the official title of host. They know when to take the initiative to make others feel comfortable in a social or business setting.

Assuming such responsibility is as natural to them as maintaining small, safe cliques is to those who have not learned the importance of host behavior.

Practice Makes Perfect

If you will soon be attending a large conference, marketing trade show, or a monthly luncheon with other business leaders, and your goal is to make some important contacts, you may feel it is enough of an accomplishment just to take time from a busy schedule to go to these functions. To achieve your goal of making additional quality contacts, however, you have to work at getting the most out of these functions. How do you begin?

Susan RoAne, the High Mistress of Mingle, advises: First, introduce yourself. It may seem elementary, but many people feel too awkward to even say who they are. State your name and professional position (to the person you want to meet) with enthusiasm.

Give enough information to lead the other person into an engaging conversation. This works well in civic meetings, such as Rotary or Chamber of Commerce. If it is a purely social event, such as a wedding reception, your relationship with the host is more important than what you do. Imparting this information takes only a matter of seconds. Practice will take away the awkwardness you may feel at first.

As discussed above, put yourself in the position of host, rather than guest. Those with the guest mentality wait to be waited on. They passively stand by, expecting to be given a name tag, an introduction, food, etc. A guest could end up waiting all evening for something socially valuable or interesting to happen. They will likely gravitate to the outer corners of the room and quietly take a seat. This may be rationalized away, by those with guest mentalities as discretion, politeness, or shyness on their part, but others at the function may view this innocent behavior as snobbery.

Hosts start conversations, introduce people to each other and generally are aware of "how the party is going" on two levels, both in what they are getting out of it, and what their guests are getting out of it. By taking on the responsibility of helping the success of the party, you never usurp the real host, but you do become an ambassador of the room.

THE ART OF CONVERSATION

Conversation itself is an area that particularly distinguishes PATTs from others. PATTs bask in the art of maintaining interest in what others say and keeping things moving. They have two major tricks up their sleeves: speaking and listening.

Listening is harder, as it means getting others to talk and then taking a genuine interest in what they have to say. Becoming a good listener is crucial; it requires ample patience and practice. PATTs encourage others to talk about themselves and participate by actively responding without interrupting.

> Timing your replies after your newfound friend has made all of his or her points will help you to reap both business and social rewards.

When practicing active listening, eye contact and body language are key. In fact, an important step whenever communicating with others is to establish eye contact and smile. Smiling is a critical expression of interest in other people.

No matter what the language or culture, a sincere smile elicits the same reaction the world over. Smiling opens up the communication channels immediately.

The eyes may or may not be a mirror to the soul, but they are the shortest route to connecting with another person.

Looking directly into someone's eyes helps to indicate interest, along with leaning forward and making appropriate gestures.

If you don't look someone in the eye, they may think you don't consider them worthy of time, especially if your eyes are canvassing the room as you talk to them. At the other extreme, eye contact that is constant and unrelenting can make the other person uncomfortable.

Sincerity, warmth, and approachability are signaled by looking at the other person just enough to show one's interest and smiling.

Following up what you have just listened to with questions is also a reliable strategy:

- "How did you feel after that?"
- "Would you do it all over again?"
- "Have you thought about submitting an article on that topic?"

- "Did you try any of the native food while you were over there?"

PATTs know that questions not only keep the conversation going, they also help to keep one focused on being a good listener.

Jackie Kennedy Onassis

It has been said by her biographers and many admirers that one of the most outstanding traits of the former first lady is her ability to offer full and undivided attention to the party with whom she is speaking. "When she speaks to you," noted one recipient of her attention, "it's as if there is no one else in the world." This capability often makes others find her immediately endearing. The same focused approach can work for you.

Ms. Onassis is also known to be a champion letter writer. She writes letters of thanks and appreciation to nearly everyone she meets whom she wants to stay in touch with. Her letters are reported to be personal and specific—no form letters or generalized statements here. Meeting her is a memorable event, and to her credit this is not because she was married to an American President and a Greek shipping tycoon.

Many a good conversationalist is a planned conversationalist. One very active socialite reports that she makes lists of possible conversational subjects—"ice breakers"—on the way to any social occasion. Besides the often overused weather, these include ideas about:

- current news events
- books
- theater
- movies
- art
- topics based on the time of year

18

Some opening gambits that work, for example, are: "Did you hear about the latest development in the Soviet Union?" . . . "Did you have a chance to see the new exhibit at the museum yet?" . . . "Everyone seems to be going away to the beach this summer."

Comments on the immediate surroundings may also be used successful to initiate ice-breaking conversation: "I just love the warm colors in this room" . . . or "I was amazed at how many rose gardens I saw in this neighborhood on my way here."

Obviously, if you bring up a new topic of discussion, be sure you have developed your own thoughts on the subject so that you can converse in an interesting and informative manner—particularly when your listeners are not knowledge-able about your topic.

Princess Diana

By her early 20s, Princess Diana, wife of the future King of England, had already developed a world-renowned capability for making striking conversation with anyone. Whether it is crew members aboard a vessel, palace guards, heads of state, or the ever-present throng of reporters, Princess Di displays a remarkable ability to make a quick, effective, interpersonal connection. She uses whatever is present—weather, electronic gadgetry, or the humor of situations—as fodder for her conversation with others. She is so adept at conversing with others at any time, she could easily give us all some valuable lessons.

STIMULATING AND CONTROLLING

The best conversationalists are engrossing and stimulating without ever seeming to be disagreeable or even particularly controversial. Rarely are they the ones who criticize an artists's work, only to discover he's the nephew of the person to whom they are directing the critical comments. The conversation goes: "What do you think of Gerard's exhibit at the Art House . . . ?"

Our conversationalist would like to say: "Unbelievably imitative stuff. It's Gauguin on new canvas." Instead, she says: "It's interesting. I need to go back and see it again. There are echoes of Gauguin in so many of the larger pieces."

Words like "interesting," "special," and "intriguing" are useful conversational staples because they are say-nothing adjectives that buy time for determining how far toward substance and candor to venture. Other tricks for buying time, used by the best conversationalists as they are forming a response, include non-committal verbal side-stepping, such as: "Ah, that's a good question" . . . or "Curious that you should bring that up; I've been doing some thinking about that myself."

These tactics, along with long pauses while taking a sip of a drink or adjusting eye glasses, buy time for phrasing just the right response. You will find that your instant, snap answers are usually not as good as the ones you could derive had you used the methods described above. Test yourself in your next social encounter and notice the difference.

PATTs are usually always in control of the conversation—and most other things, and not just because other people grant that control to them. They maneuver situations toward control by *saying only as much as they want and mean to say.* They can start a conversation on almost any topic and they can keep it going, but they are never drawn into talking too much.

Instead, they get others to talk by dodging controversial self-disclosure and posing thought-provoking questions on interesting topics. They will deftly deflect tough questions like the good politicians they are. Then, they listen while encouraging more discussion. Others go away either flattered by the interest that was taken in their ideas and opinions or slightly embarrassed that they were too vocal on controversial subjects that were deftly side-stepped by the more astute PATTs.

Rarely do these expert conversationalists enlist direct humor as a ploy. You will not catch them opening with: "Did you hear the one about . . . ?" or "I heard the funniest joke the other day." Their humor is less direct, more wry and tends toward the quick and amusing rejoinder. It is the dry comment that needs only a few words, definitely not the story telling or belly laughing one-upmanship. It is wit. Other people respond to it by thinking, "She is incredibly clever," rather than, "She is incredibly funny."

AVOIDING BEING COLLARED

Successful people often are asked for advice or information or any number of favors. This backs them into a corner when they don't really want to say "Yes," but "No" might be seen as an impolite refusal. After all, the person doing the asking may be an important client or the spouse of a close friend. He or she might be the longtime family doctor, lawyer or accountant, in any case, someone who should not just be "brushed off."

One top executive solves the problem of annoying questions asked by parasitic acquaintances by thinking of some "rather imposing assignment" to give the inquirer. For example, if collared for his opinion on a new product idea, he'll suggest that the inquirer do some research first: "That's a tough one to predict in the long term, so you'll need the opinions of other informed sources as well. Why don't you contact your friend Alex Lind at XYZ Company and Susan Stanis at ABC Company. Then let's compare what they think to my ideas on your product."

When asked to contribute to a new charity, the polite way of refusing is to ask to see several years of balance sheets or auditors' statements. "You know what a fanatic I am about researching these things. I'd like to show some of the paperwork to my accountant too. We especially need to see the information on their tax-deductibility status"

When asked to hire a friend's son, or daughter, for a summer job (any job, not a specific job), he often asks for a letter, a resume and an outline of where the applicant believes

21

he could contribute to the company. "Have your son then call our personnel department to follow-up on the ideas about how we could structure an appropriate part-time assignment for him. Maybe he could also write out a brief summer job description to give us an idea of his objectives and desired outcomes."

This executive has found that the overwhelming majority of the individuals, given these preliminary requests for information, rarely follow up with the materials suggested. "When that rare person does follow-up with what I've asked for, he or she gets my attention. At that point I have to say, 'Here's someone who is tenacious and really wants to work in my company for the summer.' Then I'll help set up an interview to determine his or her qualifications."

SOCIALIZING

Conversation is but a vital piece to the art of socializing. Succeeding on the social scene requires more, and PATTs know just what that "more" is.

It is knowing what to wear, say and do.

It is knowing how long to stay and who to be sure to talk with.

It is knowing the protocol of seating arrangements and who makes the first toast.

It is understanding that it's still okay to rely on that time-honored tradition of men and ladies retreating to separate parts of the house after dinner.

Commanding attention, or working the room, is how some people describe what a politician does when he or she strides through a crowd shaking hands, smiling, kissing babies and patting backs. Expert socializers and shrewd PATTs also strategize at social occasions, with their own objectives in mind. Some may just want to see and be seen, check out who is there, show off their new Martinique sun tan, mention that Wilhelmina Jr. is graduating from Stanford next week, etc.

Others have a more focused agenda and use social occasions as times for making business contacts or improving business relations. Obviously, some social functions are attended strictly for business reasons, as when a lawyer attends the annual picnic of a company he or she represents or when a top executive in an automotive firm attends a cocktail party given by the Assistant Secretary of Transportation.

Most functions are a melange of people and purposes, however, and attendees are left to make what they will of them.

"When I first enter the room, I spend a lot of time planted in one place near the door, just surveying the situation," says one wealthy Chicago socialite. "It's exactly what I do when I'm at the top of a ski hill, stop and survey the hill to pick my route down among the moguls." This surveying tactic gives her time to determine who else is attending the function and decide who to talk to. "If it's a stand-up cocktail party (many dinner parties start that way) and there are only a few interesting people whom I know, then I figure out early that I can spend as much as 20 minutes in conversation with each. If there are a lot of people I'll want to see, I know to limit my time with each."

People who "work a room" don't stand in one place for long. They move on to talk to new guests frequently, often with the excuse of getting another drink, in a fairly consistent pattern of either clockwise or counter-clockwise motion.

Moving On Gracefully

The tactics that some use for moving away from others are perhaps the most interesting of their skills. For example, one

CEO's strategy for moving away from a bore is to look around the room for one of his staff. When he spots one, he waves him or her over and introduces the bore with something like, "You two haven't met, but [staff person] you really must tell [the bore] all about the XYZ project." As they begin talking, the CEO will stealthily slip away, moving on to more stimulating and productive conversations on the other side of the room.

Other successful tactics for moving along are more direct: "That's a wonderful story; let's have lunch sometime so I can hear more about it. Will you please excuse me, I see someone who wanted to speak to me."

And then there's always the reliable: "Well, look who just came in. If you'll excuse me a moment, I do need to see Timothy. I've been trying to get him on the phone all week."

Excusing oneself to make a trip to the bar or restroom is, of course, also an old but effective ploy.

Act Commanding

PATTs seldom have the problem of nobody to talk to; but if left alone momentarily, they have a knack for acting in a commanding manner. Rather than sinking into the woodwork, they stand straight and, sipping a drink, they survey the room with a look of alert interest and even slight amusement. *They are never left out because they don't ever act left out.*

Often successful people don't wait for others to come to them. They have an agenda, and they are in command of it. Their plan may be to see a few people, fulfill the obligation of being there and leave as quickly as possible. Or it may be to make points with their clients, get information from a competitor, or keep a spouse happy by just showing up. It is a conscious agenda—these people know why they are there.

POWER DINING

Being at a social event is not the only aspect of socializing at which PATTs excel. They are also good at hosting such occasions, following the advice found in the protocol books by Letitia Baldrige, Judith Martin and, of an earlier era, Amy Vanderbilt and Emily Post.

When they go out to public places, especially restaurants, they exhibit what is perhaps their most obvious skill—control. Control when dealing with a restaurant begins with selecting the appropriate place. PATTs choose places they know well and patronize often. They work to become well known at a few excellent establishments, some earmarked for lunches and others for dinners. In time they even arrange to be greeted by the maître d' by name. They have a history of frequent attendance and good tipping, so they are almost always treated with great regard. They are seated and attended to accordingly.

Ron Brady

In San Diego, California, Ron Brady operates an $85-million-a-year general services construction firm. Brady took over the business from his father several years ago when the company was doing $9 million in annual revenue.

Brady has an unique method of tipping that has served him well over the years. When he brings his Mercedes into a garage or restaurant valet parking, he tips the attendant *in advance*. When he enters the restaurant, he tips the maître d' *in advance*. Likewise, whenever he is in a situation where a service is about to be rendered Brady tips *in advance*. To his way of thinking, it makes perfect sense. You want to give the service provider the greatest incentive to provide excellence service, therefore why make him wait. As you might expect, Brady's car is treated with the utmost of care, and when he sits down to eat at a restaurant he is always given the best table and VIP treatment.

25

"I always eat at the same few places," says one top executive, "but it's worth it. They know me; they like me; they treat me well; and these are places where the food is terrific. It makes me feel at home and impresses others who are with me. That just makes more sense to me than trying a new place every week just to keep up with the changes in what's in and what's out."

RECOMMENDED TIPPING RANGES

Apartment doormen, superintendent: $25 to $50 at Xmas
Babysitters: 10 percent to 15 percent of charge
Barbers, beauticians: 15 percent of bill
Coat check: If no fee, $1 per coat for the first two, 50 cents per coat thereafter
Garbageman: $5 to $10 per crew member at Christmas
Hotel bellman: $1 per bag
Hotel doorman: $1 when unloading bags; at least 50 cents for calling cab
Hotel maid: $1 per day
Locker room attendant: At least 50 cents for towels
Newspaper carrier: $5 to $15 at Christmas
Restaurant captain: 5 percent of pretax bill
Shoe shiner: 50 cents to $1
Skycaps: $1 for one to three items (more, depending on size and weight)
Supermarket bag loader: 25 cents per bag
Taxi drivers: 15 percent to 20 percent of fare
Washroom attendant: 50 cents to $1
Waiter/Waitress: 15 percent to 20 percent of the bill before tax
Wine steward: Up to 10 percent of wine bill

Who doesn't get tipped?

A restaurant owner (Just say thanks.)
Busboys (They get a cut of waiters' tips.)

Doormen for merely opening doors (Tip them when they
   help you.)
Hotel bellman, if you don't need them
Anyone on a plane

Control also means control of the meal itself. PATTs are
often the first to suggest, "We'll wait to order until we've
finished our drinks," or to recommend to fellow diners, "The
broiled swordfish here is wonderful." Several well-heeled
diners report that they make an effort to know the history of
the establishments they frequent, so they have an instantly
interesting conversation-opener for their guests.

It goes something like: "Henri started this place as a six
table take-out shop back in the mid-'60s. Then, when it got
going, he expanded by breaking out into the back. He just
added the outside deck last year when he hired the chef away
from La Provincia. He's put his son in charge of the deck."

PATTs often avoid certain restaurants. It goes without saying that getting up and getting one's own food smacks much
too much of a cafeteria. When trapped into eating at a restaurant with a salad bar, however, many PATTs still manage to
gain control. They do this by asking the waiter to do the deed
for them: "Please make a selection for me, mostly greens, with
the oil and vinegar dressing."

BUSINESS PROTOCOL

What applies to social situations also applies to the entertaining side of business situations. PATTs are determined to
stay in control. Consider the business lunch. People at the top
somehow know who should pick up the tab, and ethics are
their first consideration.

Anything that smacks of a "pay-off," through one individual buying lunch for the other, will usually result in the PATT
suggesting, "We'll have separate checks please." In most
cases, however, if one person invites another to lunch, the

inviter buys for the invitee. Any squabbling over who will pay the bill is quickly quelled by the PATT, who takes command and pays the bill.

One executive says that the key is to make it all clear from the beginning: "I'll call and say, 'How about coming to lunch with me at the XYZ restaurant,' if I intend to pick up the tab. Then, I suggest the day and time. I may even pick up my guest in a taxi. When we get there, I suggest what we should order. By the time the check arrives, it's pretty much a given that I'll be paying it. After all, I've been the host."

Conversely, if someone makes a meal date because he just wants companionship, rather than a host/guest situation, all decisions should be made equally. The choice of where and when to go should be mutually agreed to and the cost of the meal should be shared.

Those at the top *are more stingy with their time than their money.* Company parties are rarely the preferred method of socializing for PATTs. They often show up late, shake a few hands and leave. They are careful *not* to be too closely identified with the lower echelons in the organization and while they will be friendly to their subordinates, they will take every opportunity to set themselves apart with an appropriate, mild aloofness, rather than any semblance of flamboyance or display of their corporate power. Those at the top are careful in managing their mingling and will seek out others in their strata of the corporate ladder.

If there was a going away lunch for a colleague and a conflicting departmental meeting, the meeting would take precedence for the PATT on the climb. In place of going to the party, they would leave an elegant gift on the desk of the departing individual, perhaps a small calendar in a Tiffany silver stand-up frame or a sterling silver picture frame for their desk, etc.

When the people at the top do participate in a company event, even one as casual as the annual company picnic, they generally follow three basic rules: (1) arrive late; (2) drink, eat, and talk little; and (3) leave early.

When making a golf date, it is the secretary who does the calling. The secretary may make the actual social date and keep the social calendar, or she may initiate the call and then put her boss on the phone. In the latter case, an important factor in establishing control is to get the other party on the phone first, before you are called to the phone.

A secretary will be instructed to make sure Ms. X is actually on the line before Mr. Y (our person in control) is summoned to get on. After all, Mr. Y is so busy he can't possibly risk being asked to wait while Ms. X is being sought.

Business Travel

Business travel, as well as the increase of women in top business positions, has created a flurry of quandaries about the correct business protocol:

- Who holds the door?

- Who picks up the tab at lunch?

- Do male and female colleagues sit together on airplanes, or does that "look bad"?

Those at the top don't seem to have these problems because they are insulated from them in their executive suites. They don't "take" female colleagues to lunch; they meet them at the restaurant. They separately plan their flight reservations to a conference attended by many colleagues. The underlings arrive first to do advance planning and to set up the meeting details. Because of this fact, PATTs are unlikely ever to arrive on the same day. They *do not coordinate with others* arrangements for getting to and from the airport. They take their limos or corporate taxi services. In sum, they stand apart. By doing so they discreetly enhance their image and the aura of belonging at the top.

29

THE ART OF GIVING

Etiquette books spend a great deal of time and print on the subject of gifts and giving. Typically, they focus on how to handle tricky situations: the gift for the re-marriage of a couple who were divorced fifteen years earlier or the baby shower item for the mother expecting triplets. (If you were planning to give an infant seat, do you have to now give three?)

On the other hand, what is the appropriate thank-you gesture for a gift? Is a new widow expected to write a letter to every person who donated to the cancer society in the name of the deceased, or is a printed thank-you card okay when the number of contributions tops a hundred? We won't attempt to answer these questions here.

Executive gift-giving requires its own set of rules and it's something PATTs do notably well.

They know that a gift should never seem like a bribe or an inappropriately overblown thank-you. The most memorable gifts are for occasions when the giver could have gotten away with no gift at all. A gift sent to a friend whose parent just died (in this case, a poignant book is best) is more memorable and more appreciated than the gift brought to a surprise birthday party.

Successful people do not necessarily remember the birthday of each friend, there are plenty of software programs to take care of that if they are so inclined. They do, however, send appropriate gifts for rare occasions—housewarming presents for a new home, presents for a new baby and congratulatory gifts for significant business accomplishments. Each gift must somehow be special if the gesture is to be effective. Fine wines, baskets of gourmet fruits and snob-appeal chocolates are staples among the gifts that PATTs like to bestow.

Other typical gifts to faithful clients, suppliers, and long-time employees run the gamut from hard-to-get tickets to events to restaurant gift certificates. At the White House, the "in" item is a pair of tickets to the President's box at the Kennedy Center. Season tickets to a community theater company or tickets to a professional or university athletic event are frequent gift items from those at the top. The effective gift singles out an individual (as a present for an entire division would get too impersonal and lose much of the point), and either two or four tickets are sent. Any more is considered overkill. This approach strikes just the right chord, as it is neither too familiar nor too personal.

The successful executive at the top who gives gifts leans towards offering the memorable or the unusual, with a goal toward building or cementing important corporate relationships. For example, P.J. Roach, who runs a real estate business in Boulder, Colorado, thanks those who successfully refer a client to him by giving generous gift certificates for a dinner for two at a very fine restaurant. What's so unique about this? He makes sure to choose an exquisite restaurant that is approximately an hour's drive from their home. It costs a bit more in the short run, but it firmly plants P.J. in the minds of his clients, forever.

"This way," he says, "they won't be able to use it right away because the distance requires that they plan for it." As the date approaches, because it has been planned, they'll be talking about it, and "probably also talk about me." He is planted in their memory, and when the couple runs into someone else who might need a real estate agent, who do you think they will recommend?

Those sending tickets, or any other gift, know that *there are preferred ways of presenting gifts. Delivery is not random.* A gift must never be presented in person, but should be sent either by messenger (possibly too dramatic), Federal Express or U.P.S., or by the mails. It may be sent to the recipient's office if it is fairly impersonal (tickets to a baseball game) and has little "family" connotation. Gifts of wine or decorative objects for a home should be sent directly to the recipient's residence. If the gift is for an office colleague, it should be waiting on his desk that morning.

*The most successful individuals know that they possess
a certain style and reputation from their well-thought-out
gift-giving, setting them apart in a favorable way.*

Notes with Gifts

Notes sent with gifts and thank-you notes for gifts you receive
are important. One item you must never skimp on is the
stationery that your note is written on. PATTs know that paper
is a significant part of their image, not unlike their cars and
clothes. Their stationery is often extraordinary, but subtle,
with any decoration strictly in the border. Name and address
should appear on the envelopes and the paper.

The notes from gift senders and recipients are generally
sent on fairly stiff paper or cards that fit into matching envelopes without folding. This is far more personal and distinctive
than business letter stationery which demotes one's present
into an official business gift and reminds recipients that the
company probably paid for it.

The shorter the note accompanying the gift, the better:
"With thanks," and name; "Happy holidays," and name; or
"Congratulations," and name. All should be hand written as
legibly as possible. Regarding the thank-you note, this should
also be brief and to the point: "We'll enjoy using the tickets.
Thank you" . . . or "Thank you so much for your thoughtful-
ness. The chocolates are delicious."

When a gift has arrived at the house, even from a business
associate, it is perfectly acceptable for the spouse to write the
thank you note.

ABOVE ALL, COURTESY

In his book *Success Forces*, Joe Sugarman, a successful Chicago-
based entrepreneur and direct mail cataloger, says that he
learns whom to do business with by the way they treated his
receptionist. The president of one large company whom

Sugarman was trying to do business with was in town one day and happened to call while Sugarman was out of the office. The caller politely left his name and message and asked that the call be returned at Mr. Sugarman's convenience.

Sugarman noticed that this caller's manner was in stark contrast to many of the calls his receptionist received when he was out of the office. Many callers were abrupt or abrasive with his receptionist insisting to know when their call would be returned. The gem of wisdom that Sugarman learned that day was that the blowhards, the ones who call loudly and often, and mistreat his receptionist generally were not the type of people he wanted to do business with, nor most lucrative of contacts.

In contrast, the soft-spoken corporate president who left the gentle message and treated his receptionist kindly was precisely the type of person Sugarman wanted to do business with. Hereafter, when someone mistreats his receptionist, it is an automatic clue as to what kind of supplier or customer he may be.

TRADITION AND CAUTION

Aren't PATTs ever stumped about the right thing to do or the appropriate thing to say? Not often; or, at least they don't consider themselves stumped. Most report that "doing things right" is something that comes so naturally they really don't think much about it. As one rising executive says: "I'm never going to get up to leave, or even make a move in that direction, until the company president gets up. Or, if he's not there, I'd wait for whatever ranking official is. I'm rarely the ranking guest; when I am I try to consider others and leave fairly early so they can get out too. This is common sense and courtesy for those who are anxious to please top management."

In general, people on top fall back on two principles during those rare occasions when they might be stuck for the appropriate things to say or do: tradition and caution. If there is time, they will refer to a book of formal etiquette and follow tradition. If the issue is what to say or do immediately, they will get rather slow and conservative—few words, deliberate moves and lots of waiting and seeing.

For these individuals, somehow even when they don't have a clue as to what to do, their best guess at the right behavior seems perfectly proper—or at least that's how everyone else sees it.

Chapter One

Hot Tips/Insights

- Beginning well ahead of the time that they themselves reached the top, people at the top watched and studied others at the top.

- Much of the "right way" they look and act is related to a matter of degree—neither too much nor too little. Understatement in mannerisms, speech, and appearance is the key.

- PATTs learn to speak in modulated voices—which inspires those around them to lean forward and listen.

- While successful people are visible people, they are careful to not be overexposed, showing up at just the right number of social and political events, gallery openings, and charity balls to keep in circulation.

- They make it their business to be informed about what is taking place around them—from who just acquired a house in the country to who is having a baby and to who just got a promotion.

- They take the trouble to find out the names of an important business client's secretary and wife or husband and use these to strategic advantage.

- PATTs know that, in its simplest form, power between two people is held by the person *who knows the most about the other*.

- In the face of ever-changing trends or fads, PATTs often respond by maintaining tradition. They also invest in and cultivate "signature symbols."

- When greeting and introducing others, PATTs know to begin with people of the highest corporate rank and work downward—until everyone in the room is introduced.

- PATTs don't have to be the host to know the importance of taking the initiative to make others feel comfortable in a social or business setting.

- PATTs are able to maintain interest in what others say. They are skilled at both speaking and listening.

- They can start a conversation on almost any topic and they can keep it going, but they are never drawn into talking too much—they *say only as much as they want and mean to say.*

- At a social gathering, PATTs move on to talk to new guests frequently, often with the excuse of getting another drink, in a fairly consistent pattern of either clockwise or counter-clockwise motion. They have an agenda, and maintain command of it.

- They exhibit what is their most obvious skill—control—when they go out to public places, especially restaurants.

- PATTs know who should pick up the tab at a business lunch or dinner, and ethics is their first consideration.

- PATTs are more stingy with their time than their money.

- PATTs who attend company events follow some basic rules: arrive late; drink, eat and talk little; and leave early.

- They are careful gift-givers—offering just the right gift with style yet little fanfare.

- PATTs know that paper is a significant part of their image, much like their cars and clothes. Their stationery is often extraordinary, but subtle, with any decoration strictly in the border.

- PATTs fall back on two principles during those rare occasions when they might be stuck for the appropriate things to say or do: tradition and caution.

- Above all, PATTs are always courteous.

Chapter Two

THE ACHIEVEMENT FACTOR

When a man is earnest, and knows what he is about, his work is half done.

—Comte de Mirabeau

Social success can be obtained with or without personal achievement; business or career success cannot. What are the traits of high achievers and what propels high achievers to do what they do? Extended observation of PATT reveals that most, but not all, possess some combination of:

- organizational capability
- work spirit
- goal orientation
- calculated risk-taking ability
- having a gift for seizing opportunity
- personal integrity and well-developed conception of self
- personal systems and rituals

- the ability to remain unfazed by rejection
- satisfying and serving others

As we proceed through this chapter describing each of the above characteristics, ask yourself, "To what degree do I possess this characteristic?" You could even grade yourself with an A, B, C, D, or F regarding your competency in each area. It's important for you to work on developing those that you may be weak on if you want to improve your chances for getting and staying at the top.

ORGANIZATIONAL CAPABILITY

The most effective among us, particularly those who have achieved significant success in their careers, tend to have well-developed organizational capabilities. In short, they are super-organized. They can immediately find things when they need them. They are aware of the resources at their disposal and create personal systems to draw upon them efficiently.

The highly organized are able to synthesize the diverse elements necessary for high achievement: *managing people, resources, tasks, funds, and themselves.* They also create and devise systems that work, or hire people who create or devise systems that work.

Don Beveridge

Don Beveridge is a $10,000-an-hour keynote speaker for major organizations and professional associations throughout the United States and Europe. Some of his clients include Burger King, AT&T, Harley Davidson, and Toro Motors. You might think that a man with a hectic schedule who leads a thriving consulting business as well as speaking career—with homes in the Midwest, Palm Beach County, Florida, and the Virgin Islands—may not spend much attention to detail because of his extensive traveling and speaking commitments.

Yet, when Beveridge travels his carrying cases are meticulously packed in a prearranged order and all of his display and lecture materials are stocked with great care. (More on keeping up in Chapter Eleven.) Beveridge would no sooner leave his home without everything fully prepared than stand before an audience of several thousand people without knowing in advance what he would say. To Beveridge, being organized and giving attention to detail is no occasional activity.

Achievers are able to convey the importance of staying organized and on top of the details within their own company—even as their number of employees, recruits, or followers grows. Those at the top know that the people who staff their organization will be looking to them for guidance and will emulate the discernible traits and organizational capabilities of management figures who they observe and interact with.

LOVE OF WORK, "WORK SPIRIT"

The term "work spirit," developed by Dr. Sherrie Connelly, refers to a zeal and zest that she observed while undertaking her doctoral dissertation. High achievers, as a rule, have a high degree of work spirit. The energy and enthusiasm they have for their work is easily conveyed to followers or staff members. Dr. Connelly believes that those with work spirit also have a profound sense or belief that "everything they have ever done contributes to what they are doing now."

PATTs *don't see their work as work.* Instead they perceive it as fun, important, challenging, intriguing, useful, rewarding and/or productive—many different things, but not work. Many would still excel at their same job even if their compensation was drastically reduced.

Throughout history great achievers and great leaders have demonstrated great love of work.

Thomas Edison was fueled by his desire to create.

Martin Luther King, Jr., was fueled by his desire to liberate.

Florence Nightingale was fueled by her desire to serve.

Winston Churchill was fueled by his desire to preserve freedom.

Ralph Nader was fueled by his desire to protect and educate.

Today, work spirit is readily reflected in the computer hardware and software industry, among other industries. William Gates, the head of Microsoft, who is the youngest person in the world to earn his first $1 billion, has work spirit. The widely known Steven Jobs of NEXT, and Sandy Kurtzig of ASK, who took a few years off to raise a family but returned sharp as a pistol, all come to work *on fire*.

These people and others like them have never had the Monday morning blahs that the rest of the world experiences. They are *impassioned* by what they do. Workaholics? possibly, but achieve-aholics is probably more accurate.

Work spirit leads directly to another element—goal orientation.

GOAL ORIENTATION

Though it's not always visible to the casual observer, the high achievers and powerful people among us usually operate as if they have a mission—some driving force, usually larger than themselves. This goal may be broadly defined, yet it exists as a pillar or guidepost for focus or direction of all energies.

Dr. Charles Garfield says that most of the 550 top performers he studied have a goal that has motivated them to succeed. When Lee Iacocca turned around Chrysler, he was on a mission. Tom Peters, the best-selling author of management books, has a goal—to revamp, recreate and revitalize the American management system. Producer/director/writer/actor Spike Lee's goal is to bridge racial and ethnic barriers through movies, while generating personal prosperity. Dr. Norman Vincent Peale—still active at 92, and himself a high achiever—consistently depicts great achievers as people who unmistakably have a specific mission that they want to achieve.

Nelson Mandela's inspirational goal to abolish apartheid was not changed by more than 27 years of imprisonment. As he toured America in order to connect with people and honor their right to be free, Mandela donned a Yankee cap in Yankee stadium and became the first black private citizen to address a joint session of Congress in Washington.

Getting in Touch with Your Goals

Wayne Dyer, Ph.D., says you don't find your mission, "it finds you." While some people make it to the top without goals, those who get there faster and stay there longer dedicate themselves to some goal. The goal is something that comes from within, not one imposed by an external source. For example, despite considerable external pressure to follow in his father's footsteps, Ron Reagan, Jr., President Reagan's son, set his own goals. He originally studied ballet as a career and has now taken up being a radio show host and an occasional television interviewer.

Your goal may be derived from something learned when you were young, or after years of hardship and struggle. In his book *Super Achievers*, Gerhard Gschwandtner confirms that top achievers are self-motivated and create goals based on self-knowledge. A happy coincidence is when your personal mission is compatible with that of your company or organization. This creates a powerful combination.

41

Many high achievers write down their goals and create a "mission statement" as a basic explanation of what they're committed to or committed to do. A well-crafted mission statement reflects one's hunger or passion and is expressed in straight-forward terms that are easily understood. The better articulated the goal is, the greater your odds of rising to the top and staying there.

To get in touch with your goal, spend time exploring the things that you truly care about. Separate your wishes from those of your customers, spouse, peers and associates.

Do you like the variety of a general practice as a doctor or lawyer, or do you want to specialize?

As a program manager in television will you miss the everyday hands-on creativity and adrenalin flow of writing and producing?

As a middle manager in a large corporation, can you afford the personal trauma and the risk of moving your family, with teenage children, to Los Angeles, to take a position in upper management?

High achievers don't drift; they form a conclusive plan for where they're heading.

A Focus on Success Itself

If you haven't already heard of him, Anthony Robbins, barely in his 30s, is likely to become a household word before the end of the 1990s. Robbins has revolutionized the "you can do it" motivation/success industry. Originally known for his fire walk seminars and his best-selling book *Unlimited Power*, he is now packing in thousands of career-oriented individuals in carefully coordinated seminars throughout the country.

Robbins is a high energy person who goes flat out, non-stop for eight hours during his unique seminars. Perhaps most amazing, is that during the break when other speakers and seminar presenters try to visit the restroom, or stop to simply recharge their batteries, Robbins continues to interact with the seminar attendees hosting questions, taking requests, collecting business cards, dispensing personal anecdotes, until it is time for the session to resume.

With the level of effort and energy that he puts out, one would think that it wouldn't be possible for him to stay with those seeking his attention during the all important break period, yet there he is, continuing to share his knowledge during the time he's supposed to be resting.

Top speakers today receive $15,000 to $25,000 for lecturing fees. Yet Robbins has generated more than $250,000 for a single session. What is the secret of his success? A goal, a singular focus. Robbins has found out what makes people successful in all walks of life. Imparting this information in a lively manner fascinates his audiences.

CALCULATED RISK-TAKING ABILITY

On the way to the top, the winners often have to cash in on some of their chips. Some take out second mortgages on their homes if necessary, because their goal orientation is so enduring and their will to succeed so pervasive, that what would appear to be an inordinate risk to others, is simply a calculated risk to them. Taking calculated risks doesn't necessarily conflict with the notion of staying with what you know, it's a question of how far afield you are from home turf.

Media mogul Ted Turner risked much of what he had, time and again, as he launched new networks, a superstation, and the now world-renowned Cable News Network. But he knew about broadcasting and had some pretty sophisticated ideas about viewer needs.

PATTs seem to develop automatic mechanisms for gauging when they have gone too far, and when they haven't gone far enough. They are able to regroup, restrategize and attack once again with even greater energy and enthusiasm. They create their own luck by taking a series of steps and following behavior patterns that increases the odds of their success in the long term. Max Gunther chronicled this characteristic beautifully in his book *The Luck Factor*.

High achievers are not foolhardy risk takers;
they see a way, and feel in the marrow of their bones,
that the risks involved will pay off.

SEIZING OPPORTUNITIES

Risk of some sort presents significant obstacles for many high achievers, yet for some PATTs simply recognizing large opportunities is the prerequisite for success. While reading the *Wall Street Journal* one day, Richard Levy saw an article about the enormous promotional budget that Proctor & Gamble had allocated for Crest Toothpaste.

It didn't take Levy—a former publicist, Hollywood scriptwriter and marketing consultant—long to conceive of a big-wheel tricycle that incorporated an enlarged, durable plastic replica of a tube of Crest linking the floorboard with the handle bars. Research showed that every child in America in his or her lifetime will at least own or ride a big-wheel tricycle.

Levy was able to sell the concept to the product's brand manager and ultimately established a team to manufacture "Crest Fluoriders" exclusively for Proctor & Gamble. The venture was so successful that, on one day, Levy remembers having 17 forty-foot trailers filled with tricycles leaving for P&G's warehouse. "That doesn't sound like much of an invention," you might say. It isn't. Levy has the capability, however, to identify salable marketing ideas to major game and toy manufacturers who recognize a profitable product when it is presented to them.

Levy has gone on to create and sell more than 60 other "toys," some less complicated than the Crest Fluorider! He's now recognized as one of the top creative minds in the game and toy industry.

Sometimes Opportunity Is Introduced to You

Raphael Sagalyn was a literary agent in the Washington, D.C., area with several impressive, if not major, successes to his credit. In 1980, he was introduced to John Naisbitt at a party. At the time, Naisbitt was a relatively unknown consultant to corporations in the area of forecasting.

Sagalyn, 29 at the time, saw the opportunity in creating a book based on Naisbitt's unique form of trend analysis, though Naisbitt himself did not see the book potential in his work. Initially the book was to be called *High Tech, High Touch*. Leading Naisbitt through the proposal stage, Sagalyn then presented the idea to a New York publisher who offered $50,000. Sagalyn turned it down believing that more was in store for them elsewhere. He was right. Warner Books eventually offered $100,000—a large sum at the time—converted the title to *Megatrends* and went on to enjoy a worldwide multimillion-dollar bestseller.

Since then, Sagalyn has developed a reputation for seeking out projects where the eventual authors themselves may not have realized the opportunities. With *Innumeracy*, Sagalyn helped author John Allen Paulos, Ph.D., to both coin a phrase and capture a phenomenon that afflicts millions of Americans. Though the book received only a modest advance, it too, went on to become a *New York Times* bestseller.

With *The Long Gray Line*, an inside look at West Point, and the lives of cadets sent to Vietnam, Sagalyn secured a $600,000 advance plus movie options for *Washington Post* writer Rick Atkinson. Once asked why he didn't write books himself, Sagalyn replied, "Writing is too hard."

Still on the topic of careers blossoming through books, Carole Jackson of *Color Me Beautiful* learned her famous color system from a woman in California who had been teaching the system for 20 years. Years after becoming a color consultant herself, Carole asked the woman if it were okay if she, Carole, write a book on the topic. The California woman gave her consent and the rest is history.

Jackson's book, *Color Me Beautiful*, went on to be a worldwide bestseller along with her follow-up book, *Color for Men*. In addition to seizing the book opportunity, Jackson also had the foresight to enclose a reply card in the book that offered readers a free color analysis. She received thousands of cards and immediately had a highly lucrative direct mail list. Jackson's genius was to put into words and pictures a system that existed for more than two decades but that no one else recognized would be widely in demand in book form. Have you ever thought about what information you are sitting on that the world is clamoring for?

PERSONAL INTEGRITY AND WELL-DEVELOPED CONCEPTION OF SELF

Peter Royce is a multimillion-dollar real estate developer from New England. A native of Connecticut, several times per year he takes Interstate 84 between Framingham, Massachusetts, and Waterbury, Connecticut, to visit his family. Royce has a radar detector installed in his car.

Driving back with him from Waterbury to Framingham, a passenger noted that as he passed out of Connecticut into Massachusetts he immediately flipped on his radar detector. When asked why he waited nearly half the trip to do so, Royce replied, "They are not legal in Connecticut." The passenger was astounded. Here is a multimillionaire following the letter of the law to the precise second.

Among the scores of top executives and entrepreneurs contacted or researched for this book, integrity is one of the handful of traits that consistently showed up. In case you think that integrity is too pious a concept to be included in a book on power and protocol, consider this: Annually, each of us has hundreds of decisions to be make in which the issue of integrity will arise.

What effect does it have on you when you are charged *less* by the auto mechanic because not as much work was needed as was expected? Suppose you discovered that the reason you received delivery at the time the shipper said your item would be arriving was because he paid the extra express shipping charges? You'll go back to these vendors again and again —because of their integrity. Integrity has many synonyms, however, no single synonym is sufficient; trustworthiness, loyalty, virtue, sincerity, candor, uprightness, honesty. Integrity is also the avoidance of deception and the avoidance of expediency.

Integrity communicates to others immediately. It is being the same reliable person to all customers. It's not noble; it's not altruistic; but it's a practical vehicle for successful, long-term business. Sure, for every Wall Street fast-buck type who gets caught in a scam, there are probably many who don't. Then too, it's frustrating to realize that many people will go right on dealing with them as long as they are making money.

For the long term, the best odds for reaching the top in your field is to put your money and efforts into being a straight shooter. The people at the top usually get there because they can pour their energies into their life's pursuits. They stay there because they engender the support of a wide cast of characters.

The people at the top have a well-developed concept of self: They know who they are. They know from where they came, and they have a very good idea of where they are going. Many have suffered some type of identity crisis earlier in their lives. While they encounter their share of hardships, they generally have learned to smooth out the kinks, pound out the rough spots, and become comfortable with the self into which they have evolved. This is not to say they are smug or not seeking to further improve themselves, but they have achieved a level of self-knowledge that works well for them.

PERSONAL SYSTEMS AND RITUALS

Many top achievers have personal, even secretive rituals that they follow. Every year on April 26, Yoshiaki Tsutsumi, the world's richest man at a net worth of $20 billion, kneels and pays respect along with his company employee to their ancestors and to Yasuhiro, the patriarch of the Tsutsumi group. These types of spiritual activities help Tsutsumi relax and feel confident.

At Home in the Sky

When Maria Shriver was co-hosting a weekday program a few years back, at the start of each week she would leave her multimillion-dollar home in California (which she shares with husband Arnold Schwarzenegger) to host her morning TV news show in New York. At the end of each week Shriver would get back on board a plane for the cross country trip to California. Many people would regard crisscrossing the continental United States 100 times or more per year as an inordinate amount of travel; to most, it would be highly upsetting to their bodies' systems.

Shriver had a unique way, however, for minimizing the effects of thousands of miles in the air, and staying fresh and vibrant when on the air. Each Sunday night, when heading to New York, and each Friday evening, when heading back to California, she booked the same flight, at the same airport, on the same airline, leaving from the same gate, at the same time. She even reserved the same seat.

Such a system also afforded the opportunity to fly with many of the same pilots and same flight crew, and occasionally, the same passengers. On Fridays, instead of waiting until she was physically back at her house or touching down at the Los Angeles airport, she felt at home as soon as she got to her plane seat to begin the journey. For Shriver, turning her grueling ordeal into a weekly ritual transformed her seat in the sky into a welcomed sanctuary.

Early to Rise

In F. Scott Fitzgerald's novel *The Great Gatsby*, the main character's father explains why his son became successful. It was because of personal discipline. As a boy, Gatsby had written a schedule on the fly leaf of a book to which he strictly adhered. The schedule decreed the time at which he would arise each morning, and the time specifically allotted to exercise, study, work and "general resolves" such as "reading one improving book or magazine per week."

Along the same lines, one partner with a leading accounting and management consulting firm, leaves his house every day at 5:00 a.m. and arrives in the office by 5:45 a.m. Once there, he does his planning for the day, reviewing notes about upcoming meetings with clients, and setting the stage for his highly productive day with no distractions.

How much extra work could you get done if you
followed this disciplined approach?

According to *Office Products Dealer*, approximately one-third of top corporate executives in the United States get up no later than 5:30 a.m. and arrive at their offices, on the average, at 7:35 a.m. PATTs know they can get more done when they are alone in the office, undisturbed by a ringing telephone, unexpected visits by clients, or the many unscheduled disruptions that rob us of our precious and limited working time each day.

UNFAZED BY REJECTION OR SETBACK

For eight years, in the early part of this century, a young man with a dream walked the streets of Southern California. His quest was to design and operate an innovative theme park that would provide entertainment and pleasure for thousands of people. Everyone told him no one would be interested and that families preferred to go on outings and picnics.

Over this eight-year period, he was continually refused by banks and financial institutions. His family, friends and business associates told him to give it up. On three separate occasions he went bankrupt. During this time, the amount of rejection and lack of support that this man endured would have broken the most hardy of spirits. However, his dream was not to be denied no matter how many times he was told it wouldn't work.

In the end he prevailed. His name was Walt Disney. Since its origin, the total number of paid admissions to Disneyland and Disneyworld *exceeds the population of the United States*. The story of Walt Disney and thousands of others like him throughout history is not uncommon among high achievers. In fact, massive rejection is the road most traveled by self-made entrepreneurs at the top.

"Millions of people in every walk of life have never tried to achieve high goals that were achievable or solve problems that were solvable. Why? They were told or believed 'It can't be done,'" says W. Clement Stone, a rags-to-riches philanthropist who enjoys motivating others to succeed. Stone believes that anyone can achieve the highest goal or solve the most difficult problem if they motivate themselves to "recognize, relate, assimilate, and apply from what they read, heard, saw, thought and experienced."

Those who get to the top, by definition, are not defeated by the rejection that stops nearly all others. Many, in fact, thrive on it. These are individuals who routinely continue on when no chance appears left, when all hope is exhausted, when everyone else has gone home. And, when facing setbacks, these are the first to dig in, and hold the line until their goals are finally reached.

Rejection as De Rigueur

The movers and shakers of every industry face an overwhelming share of rejection on the road to what is ultimately achieved. Consider the following remarkable stories about the motion picture industry.

Paul Hogan was rejected by five major American studios which felt certain the *Crocodile Dundee* movie idea would not be successful. In 1986, the movie was finally made and released. It went on to become number three in box office revenues for the year in the United States.

For ten years, starting in 1975, Oliver Stone could not get any backing or support whatsoever for his saga of the Vietnam War. Ultimately, with the funds he earned producing and directing less ambitious movies, Stone was able to write, produce, direct and distribute *Platoon* largely on his own. The movie received 11 Oscar nominations and won four—including Best Picture, Director, Film Editing and Sound.

The producers of *Chariots of Fire* were told throughout the late 1970s by every major U.S movie studio that their 1981 Academy Award winner for Best Picture was "too dated, too British, and would have no commercial appeal in America."

Steven Spielberg has faced universal acclaim as a film producer and director, but is annually snubbed at Oscar time. In 1990, he was asked to be a presenter along with George Lucas at the annual Academy Awards presentation. They were asked to give the lifetime achievement award to Japanese director Akira Kurosawa.

Leading up to the night of the awards, Spielberg was continually peppered by reporters and journalist who wanted to known if he was irked at the Academy for being rejected so many times for nominations and awards. Being the true giant that he is, Spielberg replied that those "kind of questions bore me" and "the events are all in the past."

Among writers, tales of rejection are legion.

A reporter with the *Los Angeles Times* decided to test the system. He retyped Jerzy Kosinsky's critically acclaimed and bestselling novel *Steps*. Years earlier, the book had garnered the National Book Award and several other prestigious awards. The reporter sent the retyped manuscript to twelve major publishing houses, including Random House which originally published the book. Incredibly, all twelve publishers rejected the submission (with not one of them indicating any knowledge of the manuscript's prior history).

William Kennedy, as reported to Morrie Safer on a segment of the *60 Minutes* television program, related his experience of repeated rejection for his Pulitzer Prize-winning *Ironweed*, which has since been made into a movie featuring Jack Nicholson and Meryl Streep.

One beginning writer, as described in *Writer's Digest* magazine wrote an article which he enthusiastically submitted to several magazine publishers. After the 8th rejection, he sent out to several more. No luck. After the 24th, 32nd, 38th, he continued to send out the manuscript—he knew it was good. The 47th publisher, *Arizona Highways*, accepted it for publication. At the end of the year, the magazine's editors picked it as the best article of the year. As a result of this award, the writer was able to gain several other writing assignments and went on to launch a successful writing career.

What if he had given up on 15th or 25th or 35th time rejection? What if he had decided that the first 40 publishers to whom he had sent his piece should be his ultimate judges? Have you ever given up too soon on a good concept that you came up with? Is it too late to resuscitate the idea now?

All-Time Comebacks

On the night of December 14, 1914, Thomas Edison experienced the ultimate business loss. His laboratory in West Orange, New Jersey, burned to the ground and was completely gutted. On top of that, Edison didn't have any insurance. When asked what he would do Edison reportedly said, "We will begin building again tomorrow."

Curiously, when Edison is studied in the classroom the focus is generally on what he discovered and his dogged determination. Many people are aware that he experimented with hundreds of different items before finding the successful filament for the light bulb (over 800 in all). Fewer are aware of his major business loss, and how in retrospect, it had but minimal effect on his career and achievement.

All-time comeback honors, however, have to go to the man who signed his name "A. Lincoln." Running for Congress in 1858, *Lincoln could not carry his own district in Illinois*, yet two years later, in an era devoid of mass communication, he won the U.S. Presidency. What propels a person to run for the highest office in the land after a defeat which would have signalled to others to get out of politics? The ability to be unfazed by rejection or setback.

SATISFY AND SERVE

At the root of high achievement in business and a fundamental prerequisite for becoming a PATT is the ability to satisfy and serve a customer base or a clientele—a constituency of some sort. Robert Louis Stevenson was correct when he said, more than 100 years ago, "Everybody lives by selling something."

Have you ever wondered how some sales representatives are able to earn high six-figure annual incomes? It's not through sweet talk. Top sales representatives who earn $300,000, $600,000, and $900,000 or more per year are constantly on the lookout to satisfy and serve their customers by: solving problems, pointing out available product substitutes, helping to systemize and standardize their purchases.

One PATT continually monitors his customer's needs for more effective packaging. Another arrives on the scene as early as 4:00 a.m. for one customer who comes to work at that time. PATTs in all industries and professions keep a constant watch on the needs of the market they serve, and do their best to get there first. In business, no one achieves their success in a vacuum—everyone must cater to the needs of a buyer, somewhere. The high achievers never lose sight of this.

SATISFYING AND SERVING:
A CUSTOMER BY ANY OTHER NAME

Advertising agents call them accounts.
Airlines call them passengers.
Automobile sales reps call them prospects.
Bankers call them depositors.
Baseball stadiums call them patrons.
Beauticians call them heads.
Brokers call them investors.
Bus companies call them riders.
Car manufacturers call them dealers.
Clergymen call them parishioners.
Colleges call them students.
Credit card companies call them cardholders.
Cruise ships call them vacationers.
Democracies call them citizens.
Department stores call them shoppers.
Doctors call them patients.
Evangelists call them parishioners.
Fortune tellers call them suckers.
Health clubs call them members.
Hotels call them guests.
Lawyers call them clients.
Managers call them staff.
Manufacturers reps call them purchasing agents.
Magazines call them subscribers.
Mayors call them constituents.
Meeting planners call them attendees.
Merchants call them customers.
Museums call them visitors.
Politburo members call them comrades.
Politicians call them voters.
Prostitutes call them Johns.
Publishers call them readers.

Pushers call them junkies.
Radio stations call them listeners.
Realtors call them buyers.
Resorts call them vacationers.
Restaurants call them diners.
Retailers call them customers.
Retirement homes call them residents.
Revolutionaries call them followers.
Sales reps call them buyers.
Seminar leaders call them participants.
Software developers call them users.
Sports franchises call them fans.
Taxi drivers call them fares.
Theater managers call them patrons.
Television networks call them viewers.
Tour guides call them tourists.
Trainers call them trainees.
Vendors call them purchasing agents.
Writers call them editors.

HIGH ACHIEVEMENT AT ANY AGE

A message published in the *Wall Street Journal* by United Technologies Corporation disclosed that Mickey Mantle hit 23 home runs at age 20. Ted Williams, at 42, hit a home run in his last at bat. William Pitt II was 24 when he was elected Prime Minister of Great Britain. Golda Meir was 71 when she became Israel's Prime Minister. Mozart was 7 years old when he published his first composition. George Bernard Shaw was 94 before one of his plays was first produced. Benjamin Franklin was a newspaper columnist at 16, and a framer of the United States Constitution at 81.

On a contemporary note, Jessica Tandy won the Oscar in 1990 for Best Actress, at age 80. Marlee Matlin won it a few years before at age 21. Vladimer Horowitz played to packed houses around the world up to his death at 86. The Beatles averaged age 21 when they played on the *Ed Sullivan Show* to a then world-record audience of 71 million people. Dr. Norman Vincent Peale is still a dynamic leader at 92. Steven Jobs founded Apple Computer at age 20.

Achievement knows no age limit.

Chapter Two

Hot Tips/Insights

- The most effective among us have well-developed organizational capabilities. They are aware of the resources at their disposal and create personal systems to draw upon them efficiently.

- PATTs are able to synthesize the diverse elements necessary for high achievement: managing people, resources, tasks, funds, and themselves.

- High achievers have a high degree of work spirit, and the energy and enthusiasm they have for their work is easily conveyed to followers or staff members.

- PATTs don't see their work as work. They see it as fun, important, challenging, intriguing, useful, rewarding, and/or productive—many different things, but not work.

- High achievers and powerful people usually operate with a goal—some driving force, usually larger than themselves, that serves as a guidepost for focus or direction of all energies.

- PATTs develop automatic mechanisms for gauging when they have gone too far, and when they haven't gone far enough. They regroup, restrategize, and attack once again with even greater energy and enthusiasm. They create their own luck.

- Among the scores of top executives and entrepreneurs contacted or researched for this book, integrity is one of the handful of traits that consistently showed up.

- PATTs encounter their share of hardships but learn to smooth out the kinks and become comfortable with themselves. They have achieved a level of self-knowledge that works well for them.

- Many top achievers have personal, even secretive rituals that they follow enabling them to remain calm, poised, energized and productive.

- About one-third of top corporate executives in the United States get up no later than 5:30 a.m. and arrive at their offices, on the average, at 7:35 a.m.

- PATTs are not defeated by the rejection that stops nearly all others. They routinely continue on when no chance appears left and when everyone else has gone home.

- A fundamental prerequisite for becoming a PATT is the ability to satisfy and serve a customer base or a clientele.

- Achievement knows no age limit.

Chapter Three

READING PEOPLE AND AUDIENCES

Most people listen, not with the intent to understand, but with the intent to reply.
—Stephen R. Covey, author of
The Seven Habits of Highly Successful People

Successful executives and those at the top in all walks of life recognize the need to "read" people. They use the knowledge they gather to increase their own effectiveness, gain a competitive edge in the marketplace, and reduce stress by interacting more comfortably with those around them. Let's probe further into how PATTs put people reading skills to work.

No matter how high-tech the business world becomes, people make deals, people make products, and people provide services. All the computers, fax machines, and technical data in the world don't make a successful company, people do.

"I believe in people," explains the Scottish-born president of a West Coast software firm. "This company is people." He dons a kilt each December 31, to personally wish each employee in the company's various nine facilities a Happy New Year. While this Scottish tradition applies fun and laughter to break down barriers between top management and his employees, it also demonstrates an openness policy that they can count on throughout the year.

PATTs often are able to read others in great detail, and to recognize the importance of paying attention to others' needs. By "observing aggressively," aspiring executives and managers can learn to read people, and thus work better with them.

PATTs learn the critical elements about interacting with people that most others do not. Those at the top also realize the importance of making people they do business with feel comfortable and they transfer that knowledge into practice.

As CEO and president of Ohio-based Cincom Systems Inc., Thomas M. Nies knows that the effective company president cannot stay isolated in the executive suite of a large office building and seen by employees only in the elevator. Nies moves at ease through employee or customer gatherings, shaking hands and introducing himself.

He takes the time to establish personal contact with both the people who work for him and the people who buy his company's services. He cares, and he wants his employees to care, about their company. All the sales and advertising that claim the company is a caring one mean nothing if the people behind the scenes don't really care.

OBSERVING AGGRESSIVELY

What was once common knowledge only to behavioral scientists is now being used by politicians, CEOs, and people in the public eye to their advantage. Simply put, aspiring executives must be able to analyze the people with whom they interact to understand their needs. Meeting those needs enable successful people to negotiate deals effectively, manage employees responsibly with the least amount of stress and resistance, gain information, or enlist people to support their cause. The crucial characteristic required in this process is that of *aggressive observation*.

Aggressive observation, a phrase coined by Mark McCormack in *What They Don't Teach You at Harvard Business School*, involves working with people face to face whenever possible, since what you observe about them is more important than what you hear or read. When two people meet, aggressive observation requires that a person take action, carefully listening to the content of the conversation and watching for signals in body language.

Someone may be consciously well groomed and smartly dressed, but unconsciously hesitant, evasive or not confident, as illustrated by a closed uncomfortable posture or the chair placed far from the edge of the meeting table. A savvy executive will understand that paying extra attention to that person and trying to make them more comfortable and at ease is likely to increase their contribution, adding to the likelihood of a productive meeting.

Aggressive observation involves looking at the big picture, as if through the lens of a video camera, and taking in everything at once to decipher it later while replaying the tape. Aggressive observation is not a quick sizing up, but a careful study well worth the time spent. Since people at the top understand the importance of observing people, and therefore practice it constantly, it seems to require little extra time for them.

Aggressive observation takes practice. The more you observe, the further you travel beyond assumptions and stereotypes. Suppose on a job interview, a man speaks almost exclusively about his family when the conversation is steered in this direction by the interviewer. On initial observation it would seem that by placing his job second, this man may never undertake the extra steps necessary to become an outstanding employee.

After more discussion, however, it becomes apparent that this man's family values and sense of loyalty and stability ex-

63

tend to his working philosophy and relationships. He has devoted most of his career to only a few companies, and has reluctantly sought out this interview because of a merger affecting his department. It takes practice and aggressive observation to decide how to read this person. This demonstrates how first reactions can be wrong if they are based on too little information.

Observations must be more than superficial to be useful, they must be supported by facts. To make an objective decision PATTs look beyond the casual and comfortable observation to the whole picture. Aggressive observation enables PATTs to avoid approaching everyone in the same manner, or allowing dynamic personalities to overwhelm good judgement. By observing each person in an aggressive manner and identifying behavioral types, PATTs can work with others more easily, and more successfully. This is called "reading people," and rising executives know the importance of accurately reading people.

TECHNIQUES FOR READING PEOPLE

Gerry Tausch is an international speaker, trainer, seminar leader and business consultant. The most important skill she and her husband have learned in their adult lives is how to read people systematically. Tausch, who often speaks on radio and television, refers to a University of Minnesota study which shows that people are only motivated by their own desires and that those motivations are quite specific. Understanding these specific motivations can increase our own happiness and effectiveness, give us a competitive edge in the marketplace, and reduce stress by helping us to interact more comfortably with those around us.

Let's look at four categories of human behavior and how understanding the needs of people of each type can increase our effectiveness:

- the Detail Person
- the "All for One, One for All" Musketeer
- the Glad-Hander
- the Super-Hero

"Although the types are derived from behavioral scientists, the descriptions are in plain English," says Tausch. "Remember, too, that each of us is complex, with various needs at different times in our lives." The four types described below point out some basics about the dominant part of a person's behavior. Observing aggressively means being able to take the general information discussed here and apply it usefully to the types of people you encounter.

The Detail Person

This behavior leans toward perfectionism. Detail people ask many questions in their quest to be correct; they spend numerous overtime hours on reports for accuracy's sake and are very conscientious in every area of their work, from saving on courier expenses by delivering an envelope themselves to working over the shoulder of a printer to make sure the correct cream-colored paper is used on invitations.

Carl Sagan is an example of a detail person. In his book, *Cosmos* and the accompanying video series, one can almost imagine his dutifully writing down the name of each of his "billions and billions" of stars. Most certainly he poured over every bit of data returned by the Voyager spacecraft to positively determine whether there was one iota of proof of life anywhere but on this blue dot we call Earth.

Michael Jackson, the reclusive entertainer, has extended the deadlines for releasing his last three albums because he takes the creation of his songs and the technical production of them to perfectionist extremes, making sure each detail is, if not perfect, at least to his reluctant satisfaction.

Warren Beatty, of *Reds* and *Dick Tracy* fame, is also a detail type, attending to the nuances of production as he prepares his film for release. During the opening weeks of one of his movies, Beatty will visit various theaters to ensure that soundtrack is played at the correct volume.

Working with the Detail Person requires your acknowledgement that details are important. It is better to give a Detail Person a few exactly correct answers than to generalize about a number of issues or ideas. There's no need to be doubtful of your own abilities. A detail person will be pleased to explain details to you, once you show interest.

The "All for One, One for All" Musketeer

People who exhibit this behavior are tight-knit group members, preferring to work as a team. They are considerate of others, very possessive, and reluctant to change. They value security more than anything else. No matter how secure their position is, they will try to make even more friends in the company for a future time when they may not have the security they have now. In addition to security, these people desire loyalty and genuine appreciation from others.

Many of the large, youth-oriented food chains work under the Musketeers' principle of "all for one and one for all." McDonald's makes "join the team" a big part of its advertising for help. At Hamburger University (where employees are trained), managerial trainees can learn everything they need to know about managing a franchise and be imbued with the McDonald's team spirit at the same time.

At Domino's Pizza there are strong monetary incentives for employees to deliver their pizzas within a specific time period, creating healthy competition among members of the team. But management has also taken pains to emphasize that the group is still more important than the individual members. It takes much more then on-time deliveries to make a bustling fast-food franchise run smoothly. Catching an employee doing something right, and praising him or her (and the entire team) warmly, is key to working with the musketeer.

The Glad-Hander

These are the people who are friendly, outgoing, optimistic and gregarious. They are good in social situations and in interacting with other employees. They are often swayed by their emotions, however, and do not meet confrontations head-on. Glad-handers stand out in a crowd because they are the ones who are laughing, talking, and shaking hands. These people are frequently oriented to status symbols. Notice their jewelry, clothes, and accessories and you will win points with them immediately. They work best in a nurturing atmosphere.

The Super-Hero

This may be the one behavior that everyone wishes they could develop. *The Super-Hero is a dominant person with a healthy ego and rock-solid self-confidence. He knows who he is and where he is going.* Super-Heroes are generally athletic types. They thrive on challenges, look constantly to the future and drive hard to meet their goals. They accomplish their goals best through interaction with others.

Many top athletes, such as John Elway and Michael Jordan, exhibit this dominant behavior. Former New York City mayor Ed Koch and perpetual presidential candidate Jesse Jackson are Super-Heroes of the political arena. Bob Hope and Tom Cruise are Super-Heroes in the entertainment industry.

Give the Super-Hero challenges and access to the resources necessary to win the battle and you will have a star performer. Admire this person's perseverance and you may have a new business partner.

Being able to pinpoint the specific motivations and behavior of a person is the first step in reading people. Using this newly gleaned information helps one to better respond to people and situations.

STRATEGIES FOR INTERPERSONAL EFFECTIVENESS

"If you come at me with your fists doubled, I think I can promise you that mine will double as fast as yours," Woodrow Wilson once said. "But if you come to me and say, 'Let us sit down and take counsel together, and, if we differ from one another, understand why it is that we differ from one another, just what the points at issue are,' we will presently find that we are not so far apart after all, that the points on which we differ are few and the points on which we agree are many. And that if we only have the patience and the candor and the desire to get together, we will get together."

Over the years many strategies for interpersonal effectiveness have been successfully introduced and employed. On the contemporary scene the advice of Charles J. Givens has a strong following. Givens is the publisher of a financial newsletter, a seminar leader, a bank owner, and has started more than 48 different businesses. His book *Wealth Without Risk* was a *New York Times* bestseller for more than a year and a half.

His strategies for successfully dealing with other people include the following.

Use the four magic words: "I need your help." Even individuals who are already solidly at the top, by asking for help, can give someone else the opportunity to shine. Managers can win employees over by asking for their help in correcting a problematic situation, rather than complaining about the mistakes that were made.

A person who can't say "I need help" will not delegate or let any of the work out of his sight until he "figures it out for himself." Unfortunately, by the time the deal starts going sour, it's too late to give him the help he needs. There's nothing wrong with holding one's cards close to the vest, but being stubborn and refusing to ask for help will inevitably threaten the corporate goals and make you less productive. Neglecting to ask for help puts the brakes on one's performance, and managers will eventually notice.

Likewise, if you meet a person who just can't say "I don't know," and proceeds to bluff his way through a conversation, the tendency is to seriously doubt what he does know. A manager who can't say "I don't know" may have difficulty delegating to those who report to him—the people who do know or at least have the time to find out.

Let them tell you how to sell them. By talking, you take the chance that you have hit the one point that will sell your idea to others. By letting others talk, you give them the opportunity to describe what they want.

> *Have them say it twice.* If an employee, colleague or client is upset or angry, get him to tell his story twice. By the second rendition, the emotion will have left, and he will be able to communicate the facts. Do not get drawn into an argument. Simply listen and nod your head in an "I understand" stance. Listen to everything he has to say. By not being drawn in and getting emotional, you stay in control.
>
> Help the other person reduce fear. Acknowledge a person's feelings, whether you agree with him or not, by stating, "I understand how you might feel that way." Restate what they have said, for better understanding. "Now what you're saying is this, right?" These hand-holding approaches defuse the fears and concerns of troubled employees.

STRATEGIES FOR EFFECTIVE SELLING

As mentioned in Chapter Two, all PATTs sell in one form or another, and while many may not regard what they do as selling, they are nevertheless skilled at the process. To improve your selling skills immediately, you must demonstrate to prospective customers/clients/buyers, or whomever you seek to influence, that you are carefully listening to what they are saying. Here are three activities you can easily undertake to convey your interest:

Take Notes as They Speak

Some professionals are hesitant to do this because they think it is unprofessional. Au contraire, making a paper trail out of what others are saying compliments the speaker because it conveys the message, "What you're saying to me is important."

Restate What You've Been Told

For your own understanding and simplification, frequently repeat what the prospect or client says in your own words. Get his acknowledgment that you do have the facts straight. Use phrases such as:

- "In other words, you are saying . . ."
- "To put it in perspective then . . ."
- "Let me see if I understand this."
- "So that would mean that . . ."
- "Let me see if I can explain it back to you."

When You Are in Doubt, Let It Out

Let the other person know whenever you're not sure if you understand what he is saying. If you don't understand what the other guy is saying then he can't help you and you will have gained nothing from listening to him. This doesn't put you in a bad light; often this same person may have explained the same thing to others who nodded in agreement but later demonstrated they didn't understand a word of it.

You can often gain the respect of a person you are dealing with by leveling with them about not fully understanding their idea or position. When they are through explaining it another time then they can be sure you got their point.

Another effective approach for connecting with others is tapping into a person's "right brain." The "right-brain" (symbolic language, not precisely the right side of the brain) is that area which enables us to enjoy poetry or music, use intuition, and look past logic and rationality. Playwrights, sculptors, composers, dancers, and other artistically gifted people can access their right-brain to achieve a broader range of the aesthetic.

By appealing to the right-brain of another, whether by having music on in the background, or by orchestrating other aspects of the immediate environment (lights, colors, candles, aromas) you can circumvent layers of left-brain resistance; i.e., the "Prove it to me" attitude.

TECHNIQUES TO WIN OVER AUDIENCES

When Barbara Bush shakes a person's hand in a crowd, she leans forward, attentive to what the other is saying. This interest in others appears to be genuine, she honestly seems to care what the other person is all about. To understand the difference, compare your recollections of Nancy Reagan's demeanor in a crowd. With her single-minded focus on her husband, Nancy was never able to interact with individuals in a crowd with anything more than polite, cursory gestures.

While it's not mandatory for rising to the top, most PATTS are good performers in front of a group as well as in one-on-one encounters. In fact, many attribute their success in part to being able to handle groups. Janet G. Elsea, Ph.D, president of Communications Skills, Inc., based in Arizona, has coached top corporate executives, diplomats, and heads of domestic and international agencies on how to win over audiences of three to three hundred.

Elsea, whose book *First Impressions, Best Impressions* has been translated in Japanese, Spanish, and Dutch, says: "An examination of the basic facts about human nature, facts that meeting planners and speakers often overlook reveals that there are four basic types of audiences." These are scattered along a continuum of attitude:

- Love you . . .
- Think they're impartial . . .
- Could care less . . .
- Love you not . . .

Suppose it's late on Friday afternoon. You've been invited to speak at a convention being held locally, and the speaker before you droned on for 40 minutes past his allotted time. On top of that, the building air-conditioning system has been offering a spotty performance.

What kind of audience are you facing? "Your analysis is accurate," says Elsea. "This is a 'Could care less' audience. It has the attention span of a flea, a weekend-bound mentality, and diminishing interest in your topic." It is also a captive audience that won't forgive if you drone on, show lots of graphs and charts, ask for questions, or ignore the clock. Elsea says, "A snowball in hell has a better chance of being listened to than you. They *will* listen, however, if you can:

- be brief, to the point
- be animated and interesting
- ask nothing of them during your speech
- be available after your talk

Take that same group on a Wednesday morning, expecting a presentation that is geared to how they will benefit personally from what you have to say, and, according to Elsea, you will find them seriously interested and involved. Why the difference? "The more you learn about your audience ahead of time," she says, "the better you can tailor content and delivery to meet their needs and your objectives."

PATTs have an uncanny sense of reading their audiences, and that sense is usually backed up by homework about the audience—yes, homework! "If I'm going to speak to a group, any group," says the CEO of a Houston-based real estate development firm, "I expect to win. To increase my odds, I learn all I can about them, when I'm on, and who I follow, if anyone." Through trial and tribulation PATTs learn that time of day, day of week, order of appearance and physical setup affect people's responses, as much as the topic and the presenter.

"Because communication is the 'sharing of meaning' and not the transmission of information, it is important to find common ground and approach audiences from their perspective," says Elsea. Let's look at the four audience categories and how PATTs score optimally with each.

The Audience That "Loves You"

Some groups are friendly and predisposed to view a speaker and/or topic favorably. Effective presenters offer a delivery that is open and warm, using:

- lots of eye contact
- smiling facial expressions
- ample gestures and movement
- variation in rate and loudness
- humor, anecdotes, examples, and personal testimony as supporting material.

"With a positive audience, you can try new ideas, ask for response midstream, and urge a specific action," says Elsea. Most systems for organizing a presentation work because these are active listeners who will pay attention throughout—as long the presenter doesn't take them for granted, ramble, or use a monotone voice.

The Audience That "Thinks It's Impartial"

Though studies indicate most people approach controversial topics with their minds already made up, Elsea explains that some think they are objective. Effective presenters honor the audience's perception of itself by giving both sides of the story. Because this audience considers itself calm and rational, PATTs offer presentations which mirror that dispassion.

This group is not interested in being entertained with someone's speaking prowess. Winning presenters maintain control, are even in their delivery, but not repetitious. Elsea says that the PATTs use supporting material, such as facts and figures, expert testimony, comparison and contrasts. They stay away from humor (one might be seen as frivolous), personal stories (this audience is not interested in personal anecdotes), and flashy visual aids (such as films, videos or slide shows).

"The most effective presenters first have someone the group respects introduce them and present their credentials in the introduction. The presenters organize their material in a precise, non-controversial fashion with the sequence of main ideas readily apparent. The pro/con pattern works well with this audience," says Elsea. "With this group one has to allow time for questions and response, they like to probe and will offer their point-of-view after listening to yours."

The Audience That "Could Care Less"

In many ways, says Elsea, "the crowd that could care less is the other side of the coin from 'the audience that think's it's impartial.' Delivery is the probable key to your success." With this audience, be precise: Start and end on time, and stick to the agenda.

George Athanson, former mayor of Hartford, Connecticut was once asked to speak at an Urban League annual dinner. It was a long evening, and by the time Athanson took the stage many members of the audience were edgy. The good mayor stuck to the rules—he was animated, witty, hard-hitting and empathetic, but his wrap-up, however, left people smiling: "In closing, I'd like to make ten points. Number one, I've enjoyed being here this evening. Number two . . . through ten . . . you've been a wonderful audience!"

PATTs who are particularly dynamic to hear and interesting to look at can draw this group's attention back by varying their rate of speech and loudness levels, moving and gesturing, offering animated facial expressions and making lots of eye contact.

Timing is critical if you are going to ever shift the "could care less" audience members toward the positive end of the continuum. Try a time frame not critical to their work, such as midafternoon midweek, or just before lunch (when their attention span is high and you have a natural adjourning time). Arrange the meeting space with chairs and tables facing you, as this may discourage side conversations during your talk. Keep the lights bright, temperature low, and air moving. Elsea says that the key is to, "entertain them while being brief." Use supporting materials to draw them in, such as:

- humor, cartoons and anecdotes
- interesting and colorful visual aids
- metaphors
- powerful quotations
- startling statistics

However, *do not:*

- darken the room
- stand immobile behind a podium
- pass out reading material
- make them look at boring overhead projections
- expect them to ask questions and give responses

"Don't worry about establishing your credibility with this type of audience," says Elsea, "not only does that take time, but it also may focus their hostility upon you."

The Audience That "Loves You Not"

"This dangerous audience may be looking for chances to take control or ridicule you. It is aroused before you open your mouth, either by your topic or who you represent," warns Elsea. PATTs usually have the good sense to avoid this situation altogether, but if there is no way out, "the immediate goal," says Elsea, "is to lower their arousal levels and present your opinions calmly."

Other Important Points

Attention Span. Use facts about attention span to your advantage. Schedule meetings after a meal, late afternoon, on early Monday mornings or late Friday afternoons.

Setups. In terms of setup, put some distance and/or objects between them and you (tables, flip charts, podium). Make it difficult for them to get to the few microphones or the moderator. In short, you're better off controlling as much as you can from the outset: starting and stopping times, room arrangements, thermostat, equipment and materials.

Delivery. Delivery and content must work together. Be calm and controlled, speak slowly and evenly; speak in a measured tone of voice and with purposeful gestures; avoid random movements because they will distract you.

Supporting Material. Select supporting material that seems objective, such as data or expert testimony from their sources or from neutral ones. Avoid anecdotes and jokes since they may set off a hostile audience, but do be empathetic and concerned.

Questions and Answers. Give careful attention to the question/answer period ahead of time. If possible avoid them because you risk losing control and giving the opposition (or your competition) center stage. If you must answer questions, insist on a moderator or written questions, and never let the other side have the final word. Make it clear that you will give a final statement after you have taken the last question.

Credentials. Have your credentials given by a neutral introducer, though your best hope and strategy is to carry yourself in such a manner that whether or not the audience was enthralled by your presentation, at least you will be seen as credible.

Handling the Mixed Audience

Suppose you have analyzed your audience every which way: demographics, past experience, friends' experiences, available printed material, (annual reports, trade journals, newspapers) and talking to the person who invited you to speak. What if it now appears there is a mixture of types likely to attend?

Elsea suggests planning the content as if the entire audience were an impartial one, then stick to your prepared organization pattern and supporting material throughout your presentation. You may cut material but try not to add any. With a mixed audience focus more on delivery than content. Remember that

---

In your anxiety you may not read audience response accurately.

It is difficult to make impromptu changes in the fabric of your speech.

Cultural differences you aren't aware of may lead you to read nonverbal responses incorrectly.

It seems Aristotle was right thousands of years ago when he defined rhetoric as "finding the available means of persuasion in any given situation." That's what PATTs strive to achieve and what effective presentations are all about, whether they are at an employee briefing, a staff meeting, before stockholders, at a press conference, or at a local service club.

"By using audience-centered strategies to tailor both your message and how you deliver it to audience needs and experiences," summarizes Elsea, "your chances of establishing a positive impression and getting heard are much higher."

Chapter Three

Hot Tips/Insights

- PATTs learn how to "read" people and use this knowledge to increase their own effectiveness, gain a competitive edge in the marketplace, and interact more comfortably with those around them.

- PATTs recognize the importance of paying attention to others' needs and aggressively practice observing. They learn the critical elements about interacting with people that most others do not know.

- People are mainly motivated by their own desires and those motivations *are quite specific.*

- Ask others for their help; it's a simple, but disarmingly effective way to gain their support.

- If an employee, colleague or client is upset or angry, get him to tell his story twice so that the emotion will have subsided, and he will be able to better communicate the facts.

- Demonstrate your active listening skills by taking notes when someone else speaks to you, restating what you've been told, and letting the other person know whenever you don't understand something he's said.

- By appealing to the right-brain of another, by having music on in the background, or by orchestrating other aspects of the immediate environment (lights, colors, candles, aromas) you can circumvent layers of left-brain resistance; i.e., the "Prove it to me" attitude.

- While not mandatory in their rise to the top, most PATTS are good performers in front of a group as well as in one-on-one encounters. Many attribute their success in part to being able to handle groups.

79

- The more you learn about your audience ahead of time, the better you can tailor what you say and how you say it to meet their needs and your objectives. PATTs have an uncanny sense of reading their audiences, and that sense is usually backed up by homework about the audience.

LEADING PEOPLE

We awaken in others the same attitude of mind we hold toward them.
—Elbert Hubbard, American writer/editor (1856-1915)

W. Edwards Deming, the man who is credited with resurrecting Japan's industry from ruin after World War II into the leading economic power it is today, says that the essence of leadership begins with determining why a company is in business.

Deming believes management should not focus solely on making money for stockholders; their objectives should be to remain in business and provide jobs through innovation, research, constant improvement and maintenance. This requires a "total dedication" to productivity, quality and service, both today and in the long run. The ability to convey this to employees enables management to feel more secure and hence be more supportive toward overall company efforts.

Who Must Lead?

Artists, inventors, chefs, and lone-ranger consultants, among others, can reach the tops of their fields without leading others. For most of the rest of us, success is based to lesser or greater degrees on the ability to lead others. Fortunately, leadership skills can be learned, and the best lessons initially focus on the leader as a person; view it as a make-over on the inside.

Though the qualities and skills that make for a good leader do not always come easy, they can be acquired through hard work and persistence, just as hard work and persistence can result in an advanced degree or major career promotion. Here are some key components of leadership, among a vast sea of characteristics and capabilities:

SOLICITING AND HEEDING A TALENTED STAFF

Warren Pelton, PH.D., former professor of management at UCLA and a co-author of *Tough Choices*, studied the Ford Motor Company; Ford went from one of the largest deficits in corporate history to one with the greatest profits in automotive history. Pelton attributed the turnaround to key decisions made by Don Petersen, the company's CEO through the 1980s.

"Petersen assumed leadership of Ford in a highly uncertain, changing environment," says Pelton. "The major key to his strategy was a change in the way good people were used within the company, while having a strong objective of quality production supported by both management and the unions."

To achieve such a brilliant turnaround, Petersen asked employees how they could help, and heeded them. "As a result of Petersen's work with the production people," Pelton says, "at each stage of the assembly line production worker teams were responsible for complete and superior assembly and production." With individuals able to provide continual and valuable inputs to the production process, and hence, no longer work in anonymity, they had new incentives to do things right the first time. This new procedure resulted in a drastically reduced number of cars rejected at the end of the assembly line with a commensurate surge in efficiency and profitability.

"Petersen's second innovation," says Pelton, "was to reverse the process of new car design by putting the decision making into the hands of the engineers rather than requiring them to develop ideas conceived by the executives." As an industry first the entire design staff was able to design a car "they would be proud to drive and have parked in their driveway." The engineers then produced the Ford Taurus—a car they themselves would choose to own. The Taurus put Ford back in the profit column. The considerable financial success of this employee-developed automobile is known throughout the industry.

EMPOWERING OTHERS

Empowering others means giving them the authority to make decisions. Elizabeth Jeffries, a management trainer and seminar leader based in Louisville, Kentucky, observes that many would-be leaders get up in the morning with an unclear sense of where they are headed and understandably convey the same to their followers.

"I believe that most leaders really want to make a difference. They clearly define who they are and what they want to contribute to the world, to their organization, and to their staffs," says Jeffries, whose clients include the American Red Cross, General Electric, and the U.S. Postal Service. "Many have a deeply sensed internal need to both make a difference and leave something of themselves in our society before they depart."

When you have a clear understanding of the difference you want to make—what you want to accomplish—devise a mission statement (to yourself) to easily review and refresh your commitment. From your mission statement, you can lay out a simple action plan to achieve your goals. An action plan can be based on your responses to such questions as: "What help do I need to reach my goal?" . . . or "How will I measure what I have accomplished?"

Jeffries says that when you can communicate your goals and your action plan explicitly to yourself, it's easier to convey them to others and then to empower the people with whom you work. All workers need something to work toward. Studies have shown that people would rather work with a manager with whom they disagreed, but whom they respected as consistent, than with someone with whom they agree but perceive as inconsistent.

The more effectively you can share your goals with others, the more successful you will be in empowering them—helping them to make their own effective decisions. More PATTs are recognizing the value of empowering others. In a *Fortune-CNN/Moneyline* poll of *Fortune 500* and *Service 500* companies, 74 percent of the 216 responding chief executives said that their management styles are characterized by consensus and participation. They assert that they *rely more on communication than on command*, and often they work directly with a team of senior managers.

As a first-time supervisor or project manager, you learn to recognize talent, foster team spirit, and encourage open communication. These team-building skills do not cease in importance as you move up the corporate ladder, even though the tendency among some is toward exclusivity and isolation from the rank and file. The team-building skills that you exhibit will stand as a model for how the managers under your supervision should relate to the people who report to them.

David Johnson, chief executive officer of Gerber Products, remarks that in empowering others, his team becomes "an extension of myself. The upper and upper-middle managers are business disciples and they then proselytize and strive to win over other employees."

In another company, which produces electrical equipment, upper management lets the people who have direct contact with customers have much more autonomy than previously. In general, the recent focus on customer service is resulting in more companies and more business leaders shifting authority and responsibility down the line to the people who come face-to-face with the company's customers.

DEVELOPING PERCEPTUAL SKILLS

In a world where images (see Chapter Six) and various forms of "invented reality" obscure the truth, to be successful increasingly requires perceiving what is really happening both within one's organization and within the marketplace or external environment. To develop and sharpen perceptual skills you must talk with people, read the trade and daily newspapers, network with your peers, join business round-tables and, in general, keep your "feelers" out.

If you lead a satellite communications company that markets inter-store communication systems to nationwide department store chains, then read the retailing publications that your prospective clients read. Get to know the industry, and what their communication problems and needs are. For example, you should become well versed in the issues of stock distribution, price control, and theft control. Likewise, if you market legal software to lawyers, read their professional publications to understand their needs and concerns.

You wouldn't consider vigorous jogging on a regular basis without keeping tabs on your pulse rate and your diet. In the same way you must look at the whole picture in your work environment, with a constant eye to assessment. Examine each situation for what it is, and develop an action plan to address the problems you have identified.

SEEKING OPPORTUNITY IN ADVERSITY

After John Hinckley, Jr.'s, assassination attempt against President Ronald Reagan, which resulted in the near death of James Brady (the president's press secretary) due to a bullet wound, Mr. Brady fought to regain his physical well-being. He has since joined his wife in writing inspirational books and lobbying Congress for stricter gun control laws. This is a good example of finding opportunities in tragic adversity.

Following the Tylenol poisoning tragedy of the early 1980s, Johnson & Johnson was able to regain the confidence of the public by quickly pulling their product from store shelves and restocking the stores with a modified version of the product in new, safe, tamper-resistant packaging. They became model leaders in reacting to a serious business crisis and turned a business debacle into a public relations bonanza.

While both of these examples may represent adversity in the extreme, they aptly illustrate the point that even in the worst of situations, the true leader carries on as best he can, and finds the good that can be generated as a result of any negative circumstances.

All businesses and all career professionals experience their share of losses or disappointments. An advertising agency may lose a long-standing client, despite a record of award-winning campaigns and sales increases. Don't let past setbacks limit your future—or your present. If your business failed, or you were fired, find out honestly why these things happened, and what you can do to improve your odds the next time you are confronted with such a situation. If the adversity was self-induced, learn from your errors, own up to them and work to ensure that you don't repeat them again.

ERRING WITH GRACE

Suppose you receive the news that a major deal has fallen through, and the fault lies squarely on your shoulders. Your board will learn about it eventually, so there is no pressure on you to be the "messenger of bad news"—and after all, didn't they kill the messenger in the time of the ancient Persians? The fact is, if your board learns you knew and didn't say anything, it will be worse than if you said nothing at all.

What they will remember is that you may not have relayed the news personally, not that the deal fell through. If you are afraid to say "I was wrong," or "I erred," you are probably afraid to step out and assume the risks of leadership.

All PATTs experience their share of stumbles and falls in the pursuits of goals.

Unwillingness to admit mistakes betrays insecurities. Not to begin Nancy Reagan bashing, but nowhere is this unwillingness to take the blame for mistakes more apparent than in the differing styles of former first lady Nancy Reagan and Barbara Bush.

Nancy Reagan will not confront controversy, such as the money she spent on the White House china or the money she didn't spend on designer clothes, or the extent of astrologers' influence on her and her husband's decisions. On the other hand, Barbara Bush speaks out frankly and plainly when controversy strikes, such as on the occasion of her speech before the Class of 1990 at the Wellesley College graduation ceremony, when students protested her selection as commencement speaker because she was "merely the spouse of the President of the United States and has not accomplished anything on her own."

OTHER QUICK HINTS ON LEADERSHIP

Exhibit Leadership Qualities Now. You don't need to wait until formal leadership is yours. Take your skills and talents out into your community. Volunteer to sit on the board of an organization that houses the homeless or spearhead a blood drive during a critical time of need. Participate in Career Day at local high schools and talk to the students.

Innovate Within Your Company. Encourage the development of a wellness program and be the first to jog around the parking lot each morning. Start an intern program, and recognize employees who oversee the interns with a special dinner or awards ceremony. Encourage research and development and reward employee achievement.

Never Compromise on Quality. Some of the great American products—and institutions—Disneyland, the Hershey bar, U.S.News and World Report are known the world over, and consumers believe they can always trust that the quality of their visit, their eating enjoyment, or their reading pleasure, will be of consistent and unwavering quality.

Narrow Your Strategic Focus. Set for yourself, and encourage those working with you to have ambitious goals, but not at the sacrifice of realistically meeting those goals.

Maintain Your Self-Esteem. See yourself clearly and accept yourself as you are, with all your strengths and weaknesses. Use your strengths for the good of the organization, minimize your weaknesses by seeking help in areas in which you already know you don't excel.

Connect with Winners. In accomplishing your business or personal goals, identify the people you must know or interact with and make the effort to meet them. These are people who have already surpassed the same or similar goals. They have the knowledge and skills that you will need. Ask yourself who at work or who in your personal life will be most able to help you reach your goals, then orchestrate a plan to meet with them. It may be a person who is already at the top like the chairman of the board of directors or the company's president. Titles don't matter. What matters is these individuals' ability to influence others or to have an effect on your future.

Continually Analyze. Always consider if you are truly pursuing the best way to reach your goal. Most goals can be reached using a variety of approaches. Blissfully heading towards goals without reevaluating the steps to reach them is risky. You should also reevaluate the goals themselves. Are they *still* what you want, six months or a year after you've set them?

Handle Small Decisions Quickly. The higher up you go, the more often you will have to make decisions. You must learn to make the less important decisions quickly and leave their execution to others, so that you can turn your attention to the larger issues.

Delegate. The inability to delegate caused former President Jimmy Carter problems throughout his term in office. Carter, notorious for wanting to do everything himself, would attempt to carry stacks of his own books off Air Force One while surrounded by staff whose hands were free.

Avoid Procrastination. Postponing the difficult compounds the difficulty. If you procrastinate because smaller challenges or assignments are easier to tackle first, the large challenges may become unmanageable because of your neglect. Remember that hurdles once looked big, until you jumped them. Often those large projects become a lot more manageable once you spend some time setting up your plan of attack. Do you let days of procrastination pass before you get to the point of spending the crucial time to plan your approach?

Set High, Fair Prices. Leadership and excellence are for naught if you don't prosper from providing your products or services. Find out what the local market will bear for your product or service, and be sure to set a high, fair price.

Step Out of Your Field to Generate Cross-Linkages. The relentless and constricting pursuit of goals can lead to tunnel vision. Life has other interests, fascinations, and ideas. The more successful you are in business, the more you will need to know about many other fields. The best leaders have contacts with people in many different industries and interest areas. If you find you are spending all of your spare time with work-related people, step back and make an effort to better balance your social schedule. You will be pleasantly surprised to discover how old friends, alumni, and acquaintances can, when you least expect it, actually contribute toward your reaching your goals.

Cut Out What Is Unnecessary. If you are involved in a peer organization which takes two hours of your time each month, but you have not been getting a return on your investment, drop out, re-organize the group, or find a new group. Ditto for other activities which don't pull their weight.

Simplify! Don't fall prey to the clutter syndrome which plagues so many executives today. Much of the paper you encounter is superfluous to your career. Ruthlessly discard those unneeded files. Stay lean and competitive. Stay as late as it takes and organize your desk at least once a week.

THE EPITOME OF ENTREPRENEURIAL LEADERSHIP

Effective leadership is just as important to long-term career success in the entrepreneurial company as in the monolithic corporation. Ron Brady, with only a high school education, started in the working world as a plasterer. Along the way he acquired the self-taught equivalent of a Ph.D. in organizational behavior, another in social psychology, and an M.B.A. President of the Brady Companies, he now epitomizes the forward-thinking, entrepreneurial leader who is dedicated to leading his employees (also cited on page 25).

From 1955 to 1978, he built the company's field force that is still in place today. Starting with a work force of 200, he built his organization into San Diego's largest employer in the construction field—the Brady Companies now employs 1,100 people, and it is one of the five largest construction businesses in Southern California.

Ron's construction contributions to the region are visible everywhere: the Marriott Twin Towers, the acclaimed Horton Plaza in downtown San Diego, the Veterans Administration Hospital in La Jolla, McDonnell-Douglas, Crocker Bank, and several Embassy Suites hotels, plus shopping centers, transit systems and high schools, among hundreds of other projects.

Ron saw an industry in which no one was human reources oriented, and set about to apply his knowledge. His results speak for themselves: thanks to Ron's leadership over the last ten years, his company has averaged 24 percent annual growth, with dazzling short- and long-term prospects. Ron's approaches to leadership are inspiring and rooted in common sense and good business practice.

Ron Brady's Thoughts on Leadership and Life

"Whether we're first or last in the race, our goal is to be the best we can be."

"In any encounter, always acknowledge the other person's point of view."

"When necessary, our job also involves learning to say 'no,' say 'bye,' and say 'stop.'"

"We consider earning a profit to be more than making money; it also means developing people and building strong relationships with clients."

"People are our most important resource, so Human Resource Development is our most important task."

"Good compensation and bonus programs are only a fractional part of an effective reward system."

"Effective managers lead people and manage things. They lead by example; they do not direct heavy-handedly, they guide."

"We expect creative input at every level. Everyone is urged to seek solutions, not just point out problems."

"Success occurs when preparation and opportunity
meet. Preparation is up to us; opportunity is not."

"Values and love are much more influential than control and force and are the foundation of our organization."

"Rooted deeply in our philosophy is a requirement to
be intentionally ethical at every level. Every person
is expected to have the moral courage to stand up for,
and do, what is ethically and morally right."

LEADERSHIP AND THE M.B.A.

Within the ranks of top leadership are a growing number of
PATTs who happen to have M.B.A.s. Not to confuse cause and
effect, the most gifted and capable people naturally tend rise
to the top of their professions. Beyond its image and status
value, it's difficult to assess the specific role having an M.B.A.
plays in business leadership and in a PATT's ascent. Does
getting an M.B.A. qualify as one of the winning moves? You
be the judge on this one: *To M.B.A. or not M.B.A.?*

The Case Against

In the May 14, 1990, issue of *Newsweek*, columnist and econo-
mist Robert J. Samuelson observed that "the M.B.A. explosion
has coincided with a deterioration in the performance and
stature of corporate America." Samuelson argues, and quite
convincingly, that business schools have really become
expensive employment agencies and that they add no more
intrinsic value to blue chip manager talent, than a few years
of college basketball added to Michael Jordan, Larry Bird's, or
Magic Johnson's careers as pros.

Samuelson is but one of many analysts nationwide who
are encouraging us to take a fresh look at how we define

professional management, or leadership, and the role the M.B.A. degree plays in this. The pendulum has swung to two extremes over the last few decades and may now be settling in the middle. Until the tumultuous 1960s, almost all business leaders rose from the ranks after devoting their working life to the company, giving rise to the phrase "the organization man." During the 1970s and 1980s, business leaders, armed with M.B.A.s, jumped readily from one firm to the next, stepping in at various levels.

Lately, increasing numbers of manager/leader types are once again settling in with companies, or at least within one field, early in their careers and accumulating all the skills, experiences, and formal tools necessary to become a professional manager and leader in the field—with or without an M.B.A.

A study of 3,500 top executives by the University of Southern California Graduate School of Business found that only 34 percent have M.B.A.s and 75 percent have worked for three or fewer companies. These executives *do not rate good connections, appearance, or social adaptability as skills that were essential to their success.* They listed: *integrity, a sense of responsibility, the capability to get results, and the ability to get along with others* as the keys to their accomplishments.

The Case For

Each year nearly 300,000 people seek admission to the M.B.A. programs at leading universities throughout the United States. Another 900,000 people—particularly college juniors and sophomores—are considering getting an M.B.A. The M.B.A. remains one of America's hottest degrees—it is no "flash in the pan" phenomenon. The two-decade-old nationwide M.B.A. boom was supposed to have tapered off by now. Instead, annually more people than ever are taking the graduate management admissions test (GMAT) in the hopes of getting into a top "B" school.

Decreases in the degree's popularity have been predicted every year since the mid-1970s. Yet, annually a healthy number of applicants from a more diverse range of backgrounds compete fiercely for a few openings among the nation's premiere graduate business schools. The intensity of this competition is reflected by rising GMAT scores of successful candidates.

At Duke University's Fuqua School of Business for example, one recent M.B.A. class averaged 645 on the GMAT, representing a 50 point jump from the year before. At UCLA, in 1988, more than 3,000 applicants vied for less than 400 openings. Though normally prepared to meet the demand, UCLA exhausted its supply of M.B.A. catalogues mid-year and printed another 15,000 to keep pace with requests.

M.B.A. degrees are particularly hot among women (more on this subject in Chapter Nine.) The *Occupational Outlook Quarterly* of the U.S. Department of Labor indicates that in 1962 fewer than 300 women received M.B.A.s. In 1982, 17,069 women received M.B.A.s, representing 30 percent of that year's total. Presently, the nation's M.B.A. population is more than 1,000,000, with 67 percent under age 40. Last year, approximately 70,000 obtained the degree. A few years ago when an issue of *Business Week* honored 50 of the nation's most successful young executives age 35 and under, much to the astonishment of observers, 38 of the 50 were M.B.A.s. This represents 10 times their presence in U.S. managerial and executive ranks. As one editor remarked, "One has to wonder: how many of the honorees would have come as far, so fast without his or her M.B.A."

The Conference Board reports among the world's 300 largest corporations, 37 percent of the CEOs have graduate business degrees. Domestically, more than half of the CEOs and presidents of *Fortune 500* corporations have M.B.A.s or other advanced business degrees.

Why such interest in this degree? Lee Iacocca has called M.B.A.s "the green berets of business." To college students and those with but a few years in the working world, the

M.B.A. is regarded as the red badge of business—the key that opens more doors faster, the key to riches. Many studies indicate the substantial employment and compensation advantages enjoyed by M.B.A.s.

The Association of M.B.A. Executives regularly surveys major business schools and companies nationwide to pinpoint which industries are hiring M.B.A.s. Commercial banking, investment banking, and electronic data processing are among the leading industries employing M.B.A.s. Various manufacturing industries, accounting firms, management consultant firms, financial services firms and the insurance industry also regularly employ a healthy number of M.B.A.s.

Perhaps the greatest motivation for the degree among students is the lure of increased earnings. Many graduates toting M.B.A.s gain instant recognition and respect among recruiters who eagerly court them. Starting salaries for newly minted M.B.A.s from leading schools such as Stanford, Harvard, University of Chicago, and the University of Virginia are frequently in the $65,000 to $85,000 range. For individuals with specific expertise or business experience, salaries often exceed $85,000. M.B.A.s graduating from even middle-of-the-pack business schools, however, can look forward to salaries in the $45,000 to $55,000 range. These salaries lure undecided students in large quantities.

Increasingly, the degree is seen as the launch pad to other pursuits. Many newly minted M.B.A.s are from the ranks of health care, and the sciences. Adding business skills to one's primary professional pursuits is viewed as a sound career enhancing strategy. Some universities such as Emory in Atlanta, Harvard University and the University of Connecticut combine the M.B.A. with a Law Degree (J.D.) in an attractively packaged four-to-five-year program.

The intensity of the competition to enter the nation's top "B" schools has prompted many to turn to expensive consultants. Firms well known in their respective industries, such as Goldman Sachs and Company, McKinsey and Company, and First Boston Corporation regularly retain "business school" consultants to get their on-staff associate consultants and analysts into the best schools, and to attract new recruits.

On an individual basis, sales of books offering information on what to say during interviews, how to dress, and presentation strategies are particularly popular among M.B.A. candidates.

So, in the business world, among leaders and among PATTs, is getting an M.B.A. one of the smart moves? Based on several measures of success, the answer appears to be affirmative.

FEMALES AT THE TOP, WITH M.B.A.S

Women have been flocking to graduate business schools for nearly two decades now. A major shift is under way, however, among female M.B.A.s—they are pouring out of business schools with specialties in finance, as opposed to marketing, using this as their springboard to the top.

From Marketing to Finance at Big Blue

At IBM, Anne-Lee Vervilles's jump from marketing to finance has made her transition to senior management possible. Vervilles, 44, is the chief financial officer of the computer giant's U.S. marketing and services group, managing a $9.7 billion budget.

Vervilles was enrolled by IBM in the expensive, intensive, acclaimed Program for Management Development at the Harvard Graduate School of Business. "I'm pleased to have attended the Harvard program. If I were just starting my career, I would definitely go for an M.B.A.—I think it's a must for future top executives."

Chapter Four

Hot Tips/Insights

- The essence of leadership begins with determining why a company is in business.

- Leadership skills can be learned, and the best lessons initially focus on the leader as a person. Though the qualities and skills that make for a good leader do not always come easy, they can be acquired through hard work and persistence.

- Key components of leadership, among a vast sea of characteristics and capabilities, include soliciting and heeding a talented staff, empowering others, developing perceptual skills, seeking opportunity in adversity, and erring with grace.

- Other components include exhibiting leadership even before you've been promoted to a leadership position, innovating within your organization, never compromising on quality, *narrowing* your strategic focus, maintaining your self-esteem, connecting with winners, continually analyzing your situation, and delegating appropriately.

- Many would-be leaders get up in the morning with an unclear sense of where they are headed and understandably convey the same to their followers.

- More PATTs are recognizing the value of empowering others. The more effectively you can share your mission with others, the more successful you will be in empowering them—helping them to make their own effective decisions.

- To develop and sharpen perceptual skills, talk with knowledgeable people in your industry, read the trade and daily newspapers, network with your peers, join business roundtables and in general, keep your "feelers" out.

- Even in the worst situations, the true leader carries on as best he can, and finds the good that can be generated as a result of any negative circumstances.

- If you are afraid to say "I was wrong," or "I erred," you are probably afraid to step up and assume the risks of leadership. All PATTs experience their share of stumbles and falls in the pursuits of goals. Unwillingness to admit mistakes betrays insecurities.

- The relentless and constricting pursuit of goals leads to tunnel vision. The more successful you are in business, the more you will need to know about many other fields. The best leaders have contacts with people in many different industries and interest areas.

- Effective leadership is just as important to long term career success in the entrepreneurial company as well as in the monolithic corporation.

- Getting an M.B.A. still makes good sense to increase one's odds of making it to the top in business, and many women are getting M.B.A.s as part of a long-term strategy to ascend the corporate ranks.

PART II

PLAYING TO WIN

Chapter Five

LIFE IS NEGOTIABLE

Where there is a will there is a way.

—English proverb

If there's one thing PATTs learn well on the road to the top, it is that, short of death and taxes, almost everything else in life is negotiable—particularly deals. They are negotiating every day, representing management's side in a union contract or deciding where to go for dinner, taking over a new company or simply bidding for a new contract.

Negotiating is all around us, in all situations. Your local government officials bargain with each other to keep your streets plowed of snow, to enact changes in zoning laws, to allow a shopping center to be built nearby, or to assess your property taxes. State and federal government officials debate what will be spent on your children's education, your community's drug rehabilitation programs, and again, the amount of taxes you will pay.

In a global sense, the 1990s could well be the decade of negotiation. After all, entire nations are rethinking the way they govern. Concrete steps toward reform are taking place on all continents, from changes in the balance of power of the Communist Party in the Soviet Union, to the emerging democracies of the Eastern Bloc countries, to the challenge to abolish apartheid in South Africa.

Learning to negotiate means understanding that the best way to get your way is to make sure the other person walks away with some of what he or she needs. There is no one magic formula to successful negotiation, but solving the other person's problems or making him think you have, probably comes the closest.

NO SUBSTITUTE FOR PREPARATION

All skilled negotiators do their homework. Chester Karrass, Ph.D., Gerald Nierenberg, Ph.D., and other top negotiation trainers agree that the best negotiators are well prepared before ever entering into the negotiation process. They establish an objective, "what do I seek to accomplish?" The answer may be obvious but the question needs to be asked nevertheless.

Another component of negotiation preparation is to examine your strengths—what advantages do you have? Financial, strategic, perceptual, geographic, etc. Then determine in advance what you really want to get from the negotiation and for what you will settle. The other party may be receptive to your ideas; hence your good ideas are negotiating tools.

TACTICS AND STRATEGY

How does one negotiate successfully to get what he or she wants? Effective negotiators make tactical decisions before entering into the negotiation process—to negotiate as an individual or as a team? This depends largely on the importance of the negotiation, the time frame and the skills required to successfully close the deal. The advantages to using a single negotiator include the following:

- preventing a "divide and conquer" strategy by opponents
- demonstrating that you have complete responsibility
- eliminating a weakening position resulting from differences of opinion among team members
- facilitating on-the-spot decision making, particularly in the area of granting or receiving concessions

When selecting a negotiating team, each member should have a specific function, know the agreed upon strategy and objectives, have a specialty and demonstrate his confidence. Everyone plays a significant role on a negotiating team; potential conflict or misunderstanding must be overcome well in advance of the negotiation.

In many ways negotiation is like a poker game; you don't really reveal the cards until after you have won. When you first start negotiating it is not wise to reveal the exact terms that you want. Usually at the beginning of a negotiation both the buyer and seller will state what they are seeking and usually these positions seem unreasonable to one another.

Throughout the course of the negotiation each side will make counter proposals and concessions until, hopefully, mutually agreeable positions are reached. Ask for more, recognizing that the resulting compromises will eventually come closer to your initial unrevealed position.

COUNTER-TACTICS

Roger Dawson, author of *You Can Get Anything You Want, But You Have to Do More Than Ask*, observes that unless you become proficient in the fundamentals of negotiation, you'll be subject to the negotiating training and techniques of others, which means you probably won't be very effective.

One key negotiating tactic, for example, which your opponent may have been taught is what Chester Karrass calls the "double finch." If you quote a price, the other party has been taught to say, "Holy cow," or its equivalent. If your opponent is part of a team, both he and others will say it distinctly and within your ear shot.

Another strategy opponents may throw at you is not addressing the issue of price, particularly after you have made a quote. This tends to raise your anxieties and put pressure on you. The other guy knows darn well what price you quoted and that you are interested in getting some kind of confirmation. His measured reluctance in giving you that confirmation is all part of a master plan.

Dawson says that if you're not aware of these types of tactics you are likely to buckle under on your price or on some other major provision perhaps only moments before you were about to get what you asked for.

YOUR BOTTOM LINE

One way to avoid the other party's negotiation tactics is to predetermine your walk-away terms—the point you leave rather than make a bad deal. So, before entering the negotiation you must determined your "bottom line terms," under which you cannot go because to do so would cause you to only break even, lose money or suffer in some other way.

Finally, always be ready to present a counter proposal —PATTs have the foresight to do this; many people don't. During negotiations it may be difficult to accurately assess the impact of suggested positions. Anticipate these before negotiating so you know what the net effect of an alternative will be. Perhaps, dividing your proposition into three separate parts will be more palatable for all concerned. The negotiator who comes to the table with a useful counter proposal often saves a failing deal and has a feather in his cap.

TIMING CAN BE EVERYTHING

Sometimes it isn't *how* you negotiate, but *when* you negotiate. When the reunification of Germany was just days away, garbage collectors in East Germany went on strike to protest wages in their nonconvertible Communist bloc currency that were far below their Western counterparts. After only three days of negotiations—not long for such a complicated situation—their demands for 33-percent raises across the board were met.

Negotiation trainer Herb Cohen suggests that one of the best tactics for assuring a successful negotiation is to figure out or estimate in advance the time constraints or deadline that your opponent faces. People are more agreeable when facing a tight deadline. However don't let your opponent know that you know his deadline! This can derail your negotiations as resentment and emotions enter into your business dealings.

POSITIONAL NEGOTIATION AND ITS CONSEQUENCES

A case of union versus management is a classic example of the most common type of negotiation, called positional negotiation. Each person or group takes a position, argues to defend that position, and makes concessions to reach a compromise.

The problem with positional negotiation is that it may not always result in the best solution. People who take a firm position and bargain from that one stronghold tend to box themselves into a win/lose situation. Many unions lost ground in the 1980s, from air traffic controllers to Greyhound bus drivers, using rigid positional negotiations. Many companies, such as Eastern Air Lines, also went into bankruptcy as a result of union strikes combined with financial problems and poor management.

Positional negotiation forces people to focus on the mechanics of the process, and not on the real issues that affect each bargaining side. In the acquisition feeding frenzy of the 1980s, when many companies were swallowed up by larger companies looking for growth, the smaller companies (described in business reports as "positioned for takeover") were soon stripped of their best assets and put on the sales block again. In some instances, the acquisition may actually have put the parent company in a vulnerable position for being taken over and the smaller company was again swallowed up, along with the parent company, by an even bigger conglomerate.

The Captain Kirk Touch

One of the reasons that fans were attracted to the television series *Star Trek* was that the show contained elements of logic, debate and positional negotiation. Each episode involved Captain Kirk or Mr. Spock opening communication with intergalactic pirates or aliens. The *Enterprise*'s position, as mandated by Star Fleet Command, was not to interfere with the inhabitants or strange life forms.

If attacked or challenged to make a move, the *Enterprise* did so with caution. Mr. Spock's logical responses were often likened to the three dimensional game of chess he liked to play. Of course, each negotiation took as long as a one-hour show, with commercials. Imagine a professional chess match or contract negotiation taking a single hour—it doesn't happen.

Positional negotiation is like chess—it takes a long time to complete the moves as each side successively takes and then gives up a series of positions until one side wins. Trainer Neil Rackham says that the best negotiators carefully listen to the points presented by the other side. Then they attack those points, indicating that they listened and understood what the other side said, that they agree in part with some of the points made, but they disagree with "X,Y,Z"; and here is why: Captain Kirk's method.

This is far superior, believes Rackham, than politely listening to the other party and then launching full scale into what you want to say without addressing and sticking with what your opponent has just said. The best negotiators choose their words and tone of voice carefully, and pose questions in a way that does not offend. Good negotiators both have notes prepared and take notes during the negotiations.

Arguing over positions, however, or maintaining an unyielding stance damages chances for a long-term relationship between both parties as the negotiation protracts. One only need look at conflicts that have raged for years between the Catholics and Protestants in Northern Ireland, or the Jews and the Palestinians in the Middle East, to see that each group's rigid stance strains the possibility of ever reaching a compromise. With more than two parties, negotiations can be even more complicated and confusing. This is exemplified by the negotiations and unresolved conflicts between the various leaders of the Arab bloc nations.

FROM POSITIONAL TO PRINCIPLED NEGOTIATION

In their bestselling book *Getting to Yes: Negotiating Agreement Without Giving In*, authors Roger Fisher and William Ury explain how the method they have developed, principled negotiation, is more effective than positional negotiation. The authors use four points to define positional negotiation.

First, principled negotiation addresses not only the problem, but the people behind the problem. Second, the method focuses on satisfying the underlying interests of both parties rather than examining positions. Principled negotiation encourages both sides to brainstorm to generate a variety of possibilities before making any final decisions. Finally, the method requires the use of objective criteria in reaching a fair solution that is agreeable to both sides. Let's explore these four points in detail.

SEPARATE THE PEOPLE FROM THE PROBLEM

It's easy to get emotionally involved when you are trying to get something that is important to you. For example, a developer wants to get a zoning law changed in order to build a new shopping center. The developer wants to do his or her job efficiently and inexpensively without complications, and feels that the shopping center will be beneficial in bringing goods and services closer to where people live. Those people may feel the new shopping center will also bring traffic, crime, noise, and higher taxes. A city council meeting can get very heated when the emotions of both sides come into play.

In principled negotiation, first you realize that you are working with real people, not "a developer" or "the community," but actual human beings. You separate the people from the problem putting yourself in their shoes, and writing down or repeating orally to others your understanding or perception of how they feel. If you were a developer trying to do your job, how would you go about it? If a shopping center was to be built next door to your home, what would you do?

If the community perceives a developer as cold and money-hungry, then the developer should take every opportunity to portray himself as warm, caring and concerned about the quality of life in the community. By making people in the community a part of the process early on, the developer can help them feel that they have a stake in the outcome.

He could attend community meetings at the first opportunity to reveal the shopping center plan and ask for input. By taking the initiative, and making the first step to include the other side, he builds a working relationship, and reduces the likelihood of future problems. A solution may be as simple as putting up a roadside wall to cushion the sound, or adding more parking lot space devoted to commuter parking.

In the movie *Five Easy Pieces* there is a classic negotiation scene in which Jack Nicholson, seated in a diner with three others, asks a veteran waitress for a special order. The waitress balks, saying there are "no substitutions." Because the waitress condescends to him, Nicholson treats her as he does other establishment or authority figures, and insults her by telling her where she can put the chicken that he doesn't want to order just so he can get wheat toast with no butter.

If the two characters had separated themselves as people from the problem, he might have gotten his order the way he wanted it and she would have avoided having to deal with an unhappy customer (but the scene would not have been as funny).

At times, just saying, "I understand how you might feel that way. . . ." and then explaining how you feel, can often lead to a mutually satisfactory conclusion. Allow people on the other side to express their emotions, but don't attempt to react to any wild outbursts. Communicate by first listening to what is being said, and then acknowledge both the words and the emotion of what they have said. You may even restate it, by saying, "Let me understand this. What you're saying is . . ." Then, listen for their confirmation of your understanding. (See Chapter Four.)

In the same way, when you negotiate, speak to be understood. Actively seek the understanding of people on the other side by asking them to restate what you have said.

FOCUS ON INTERESTS, NOT POSITIONS

Suppose, you are on the senior management team of a large corporation with many retail locations across the United States. After five years of decentralization, the president decides that the management system is not working out, and is looking to his senior managers for a new direction. You've been in charge of the decentralization and feel strongly attached to the position, not only because the failure of the decentralization might reflect badly on you, but because you really feel that decentralization is the only way for the company to keep costs down and stay competitive in the retail market.

Others on the senior management team feel that the tide has shifted and they want to jump on the centralization band wagon, knowing it will mean more responsibilities—and power—for them. What do you do?

First, look beyond your position and the opposing one to the interests of the people and the company involved. In that way, you will discover that there are several ways to satisfy one interest. Also, common interests can often be found behind opposing positions. In favoring decentralization, you are interested in saving the senior managers at the headquarters office from the time-consuming, day-to-day management concerns. You are also interested in keeping overhead costs—such as headquarters staff—down so that more profits can be realized.

In favoring centralization, the other senior managers are interested in more control at the senior management level. They want to keep a tighter handle on problems in the field so that they can be resolved quickly and decisively. They are also interested in saving money, however, so that more profits can be realized.

Having examined the interests of both positions, you might suggest a solution that would meet both interests—by proposing a network of computers at each work location, linked by satellite, that would allow better communication between headquarters and each store. The result would be better information and control from the top, without centralization, and immediate response to problems in the field—such as better inventory control and uniform pricing—to keep costs down and profits up.

In separating people from their problems, it is always well worth your time to analyze the other person's position to discover his interests. Also, understand that while each side has many interests, the most significant ones can be boiled down to the basic needs everyone has: to be secure, to be recognized, and to have a sense of belonging, among other things.

GENERATE A VARIETY OF POSSIBILITIES BEFORE DECIDING

The more you can brainstorm about a situation before you sit down at a bargaining table, the more options you will have to offer the other side that may benefit both negotiating parties. To illustrate, let's say you are on a committee to hire a new chancellor for a major university. The qualified candidates number in the hundreds, and you have spent several months with your colleagues weeding through resumes and references, interviewing people, and bringing them back to your university for additional interviews.

The field is finally narrowed down to the five top candidates. How does your committee choose one person, especially if the vote is split evenly between two or three of the candidates?

After months of involvement, brainstorming is a good way to set yourself free to see the candidates in a different light. Choose a setting other than your regular meeting place, and make it informal. As the group brainstorms, have someone act as facilitator to write down each committee member's pros and cons for each of the candidates. Match these pros and cons against your final criteria on what the job of chancellor entails.

On paper, put each of the five candidates in a number of challenging situations and predict, based on the information gathered in your interviews, how they would react. What if the university faced an educational crisis? What if a major contributor pulled his or her financial support? What if in-state enrollment suddenly dropped? Generate scenarios and see how each candidate would react. Your top candidate will

111

eventually emerge and the final vote will be much more decisive.

BASE RESULT ON SOME OBJECTIVE STANDARD

Because there will always be differences and conflicts in the way you and another person in a negotiation view things, no matter how much you attempt to understand their feelings, you should insist that the result of the negotiation be based on some objective standard or criteria.

For example, you are a project manager working on a fixed-price contract to automate the record keeping for a major corporation and the contract calls for you to complete the first phase by a certain date. However, once you begin the job you discover hidden obstacles to completing the first phase—things that the client was aware of but did not tell you at the time of your bid.

You could compromise the quality of your automation program and deliver on time, or you could begin to communicate with the client that concessions have to be made. Commit yourself instead to reaching a solution that is based on an objective mutually beneficial standard, not on pressure to complete a job by an arbitrary contract date.

The more you bring your honesty and expertise into the open to solve a particular problem, the more likely you will deliver a system that is exactly what the client wants, within a reasonable time period. Better yet, develop the objective criteria and write it into your job proposal from the outset, so that it is in the language of your contract that if certain principles are not upheld, the final product or service will have to be delayed, and spell out those principles.

TEACHING YOURSELF HOW TO NEGOTIATE

Principled negotiation is an effective alternative to positional negotiation. The best way to get what you want, however, is to discover your own style. Most PATTs do their best learning and self-improvement while observing others. Pinpoint those achievers whom you consider to be expert negotiators, and study their techniques. Then in the coming weeks take every chance you get to try your hand at striking increasingly better deals. Following are additional ideas to get you started.

Make a Good-Will Gesture

Many successful negotiations have begun with a concession —anywhere from being the first to request a meeting of both sides and then providing the meeting place and refreshments, to actually giving in to part of the other side's demands (however small you perceive the concession to be).

Create Demand

Recognize how to take advantage of a simple human truth—we often want something because it is in demand by someone else. The rare suddenly becomes precious. To the degree you can convey the potential interest of parties not present in a negotiation—you increase your negotiating edge. In the same way, the man or women who plays hard to get, but not too hard to get, is, in a manner, effectively creating demand for themselves in the eyes of the opposite sex.

Use Facts to Back Your Claims

In a court, an attorney may bring in an expert, for example a car mechanic, to back up the client's claim that the brakes on his car were faulty when an accident occurred. Likewise,

113

when you are negotiating, establish your claims and credibility by showing your expertise, or having others present who can share their expert knowledge relating to the matter being negotiated.

An example of this is when a contract calls for a job to be performed in a certain specific manner, and you have present proof from previous, similar jobs that such a manner was unsuccessful.

Be Wary When Representing Yourself

If you have a low self-image or are simply feeling down temporarily, you won't think enough of yourself to negotiate effectively. Conversely, a healthy self-image may cause you to be somewhat overzealous or overly concerned in a negotiating situation. That's probably why asking for a raise was so difficult—in the past!

TURN THE TABLES

When in doubt, focus on interests rather than positions. If you look for the concepts that the other person values, such as cost-containment or quality, and try to relate to those values, you will be much more successful at negotiation than if you perceive the other person as being on the other side of a wall and try to knock that wall down.

In exploring your negotiation skills, turn the tables by focusing on the person you are going to be negotiating with, instead of on yourself. If you are trying to negotiate a raise, for instance, it is to your advantage to know as much as possible about your opponent as well as the current status of the company. Nothing is worse than trying to close a deal on the day the other guy's New Jersey plant burned down or is forced to lay off several employees, unless those scenarios somehow motivate the other guy to want to negotiate. While you can't always have this type of up-to-the-minute information, you can sense the atmosphere around such troubled times.

After all is said and done, the fastest way to master negotiation skills is to *actively begin looking for* the multitude of opportunities that occur each day to negotiate for more favorable terms and to start giving them your best shot.

Chapter Five

Hot Tips/Insights

- While there is no one magic formula to successful negotiation, solving other people's problems or making them think you have, probably comes the closest.

- Top negotiation trainers agree that the best negotiators are well prepared before ever entering into the negotiation process. They establish an objective, "What do I seek to accomplish?"

- A key component of negotiation preparation is to examine your strengths—what advantages do you have? These could be financial, strategic, perceptual, geographic, etc.

- When you first start negotiating it is not wise to reveal the exact terms that you want. Initially, both buyer and seller will state what they are seeking and usually these positions seem unreasonable to one another.

- The best negotiators choose words and tone of voice carefully, and pose questions in a way that does not offend. They both have notes prepared and take notes during the negotiations.

- Principled negotiation addresses not only the problem, but the people behind the problem, focuses on satisfying the underlying interests of both parties rather than examining positions, encourages both sides to brainstorm to generate a variety of possibilities before making any final decisions, and requires the use of objective criteria in reaching a fair solution that is agreeable to both sides.

- Sometimes saying, "I understand how you might feel that way. . . ." and then explaining how you feel, can lead to a mutually satisfactory conclusion.

- The more you can brainstorm about a situation before you sit down at a bargaining table, the more options you will have to offer the other side that may benefit both negotiating parties.

- When in doubt, focus on interests rather than positions. If you look for the concepts that the other person values, such as cost-containment or quality, and try to relate to those values, you will be much more successful at negotiation than if you perceive the other person as being on the other side of a wall and try to knock that wall down.

Chapter Six

THE EYE OF THE BEHOLDER: THE POWER OF IMAGE

It is the dim haze of mystery that
adds enchantment to pursuit.
—Antoine, Comte de Rivarol
(1753-1801)

The transformation of Lt. Colonel Oliver North's public image through orchestrated testimony illustrates how an effective public relations strategy can swiftly alter our view about anyone and anything. While we may not find this pleasing, projecting the right image is taking on increasing, not decreasing, importance, even as business and society becomes more sophisticated.

North's performance at the Senate subcommittee hearings during a one-week period in July 1987 turned him into an American folk hero. During his testimony, North daily received thousands of telegrams from well wishers. Though he is married, hundreds of women sent him marriage proposals. Major newspapers reported that men "were moved with his magnetic presence." He was the popular choice of discussion topic at lunch counters and dinner tables across the country.

The viewing audience was not aware of the behind-the-scenes work which made North a striking, admirable figure to Americans. North's personality and appearance in his U.S. Marine Corps uniform with all of his medals and ribbons were part of a public relations "coup of remarkable proportions" according to Jonathan Blum, managing partner in the Singapore office of Ogilvy and Mather Public Relations.

What made this such an enormous feat is that most people were not aware that the Iran-Contra Investigation was going to be televised. They had perhaps read of North in the newspapers, but were unable to form a particularly clear image of him, unless it was one of some "half-crazed general wheeling and dealing around the world."

The moment he began speaking, the phones across the country lit up. "You have to see this guy," a friend tells another, during the first day of North's testimony. "He's amazing." Following his triumphant television appearance, the man in the street could be heard saying, "No matter what Oliver North did, you've gotta admire his candor and sincerity." Or, "He did what he believed was in the best interests of the country."

Many people simply became mesmerized with the testimony, many of the same people who never read the opinions of George Will, David Broder, Ellen Goodman, William Buckley or Tom Oliphant; who never watched news analysis programs such as *Face the Nation, This Week with David Brinkley,* or *Meet the Press*; who never even glance at *Atlantic, Washington Monthly, Harper's,* or *U.S. News & World Report.*

In our television-dominated media society, we've created the image junkie—those quick to judge based on limited information and the efforts of "spin doctors," those easily influenced by carefully crafted images, particularly recent images. They are often under-informed in one direction, and then misguided in the opposite direction. What's worse, we're all becoming instant judges based on 30-second sound-bites. "Washington is now divided into two classes," adds Capital supergossip Diana McLellan, "people who are trained in personal presentation and who are video savvy, and *all the others.*"

THE SNAP DECISION

Robert Cialdini, Ph.D., author of *Influence: The Psychology of Modern Persuasion*, found that the avalanche of choices confronting most individuals, combined with the information overload they experience in their daily lives has forced many people to take short cuts or quicker routes to decision making and judgment. In determining the underlying principles that cause us to say "yes" when confronted with an effective presentation, he researched hundreds of sales training sessions.

Cialdini says, "We respond to trigger features such as friendship, commitment, consensus, authority and obligation." These features "tell us almost automatically when we can correctly say 'yes' to a request." Cialdini found that the people who are effective at influencing others, as well as the most effective sales training programs, incorporate such trigger features into their presentations—which means *the techniques to instantly and favorably influence others can be learned by just about anyone.* And like it or not, cultivating the right image, sadly, often dwarfs one's substance, when being judged by others.

So, how did Oliver North trigger the right image?

Few people may realize it, "but North benefitted by astute public relations counseling," says Blum, "helping him to reverse a largely negative public image to one of warrior, defender of liberty, and patriot."

Blum points out several examples of astute public relations during North's testimony:

Personal Appearance. North always wore his U.S. Marine Corps uniform with all his medals and ribbons, a symbol that evokes feelings of duty, service, and sacrifice in most Americans.

Personality. North projected sincerity and frankness while being respectful and attentive. Also, he kept cool while under fire by the too-aggressive Senators and lawyers.

Visuals. North used many examples: a photo of himself standing beside a stack of committee documents as tall as he is; an enlarged magazine story on Abu Nidal, displayed when North discussed death threats made against him by the terrorists; and a stack of supportive telegrams, placed on the witness table.

Media Management. North was careful to make public comments on substantive issues only while testifying before the committee. Meanwhile, he exchanged pleasantries and small talk with the press outside the hearing room, which were broadcast frequently to the public.

The "Underdog" Appeal. North and his attorney played off the Irangate hearings' imposing nature to portray North as an underdog all-American hero and to stymie the proceedings. Political consultant Irving Rein, a Northwestern University professor observed, "When pressed, North would go into a monologue about America: 'I've got to deal with bad people because I have to protect America.' When he got in a tough situation, he'd turn to his lawyer and break the line of questioning." In short, North struck in most Americans what is called "the responsive chord" by evoking pathos, or compassion and sympathy for his cause. And while North had the distinct advantage of directly communicating through "live" television, Blum suggests that *anyone* can employ some of the same public relations techniques that North did, such as the use of . . .

Personality

David Ogilvy, founder of Ogilvy & Mather Advertising and Public Relations Group, and dean of the image makers, considers personality the key to successful image building. "Be enthusiastic and well-briefed on the subject matter," he says. "Maintain eye contact, scan the audience, and periodically focus on a friendly face in the crowd. Avoid gratuitous comments such as, 'It's a pleasure to be here.'"

Media Management

Attempt to establish a good rapport with reporters. During testimony, avoid "off-the-cuff" remarks. Answer questions in a straightforward manner and don't be goaded into responding if you are unsure of the correct answer. Emotional displays are usually counterproductive, even if justified.

Visuals

Use graphics sparingly, and only if they are quality reproductions, preferably colorful and are needed to make an important point. However, be aware of television's highly visual nature and try to make "visual statements" when appropriate. *The public considers television the most credible news source because viewers can "see it for themselves!"*

These are but a few of the elaborate prescriptions for dramatic and effective image building. With all that's come out since the trial of Oliver North, many people do not know now what to make of him. "When I learned how North's television image was concocted, I felt manipulated," one Capitol Hill staffer revealed, "but, from the president on down, I intermittently remember that receiving public relations counseling is a common practice." Most others, who know what they "saw on television," remain unchanged in their positive assessments.

MEET THE PRESS . . . ON YOUR TERMS

The ability to effectively manage one's image is universally recognized as a prerequisite for achieving one's desired effects. When Soviet First Secretary Mikhail Gorbachev visited the United States in 1987—two years before the sweeping changes in the Soviet—he arrived highly skilled in Western public relations and image management techniques. At one point during his motorcade through Washington, he jumped out of his limousine and took the time to shake hands with several bystanders along a roped-off area—in full view of the television cameras, of course.

This public relations gesture served its purpose well. The incident was broadcast on all of the evening news programs. It was also replayed frequently on local news broadcasts, news briefs, and news and information talk shows.

Following his visit, Mr. Gorbachev's approval rating among Americans, based on a Roper Organization public opinion poll, shot up to the highest level that any Soviet leader has ever enjoyed in this country—*and this was before* the Soviet Union's transition to a more democratic society was known.

The lessons for future PATTs is clear, you can't fight it so you might as well join in—get thee in front of a video camera—and practice your lines.

WINNING ON CAMERA

Former television news and radio reporter Karen Kalish, now head of Kalish Communications, a Washington, D.C.-based communications firm that provides training programs and instructions on being effective on camera, observes that giving an interview is a glorious opportunity to get your point across and gain high visibility. It's a chance for exposure and free advertising, to inform the public and express your views, and to put your firm in the minds of "targets." You have to be prepared, however, and that means going into an interview with an agenda.

Kalish says your goal should be to make three positive points in any interview situation. Interviewers will have their own list of questions to ask, but you can't assume they'll be the "right" questions. *You have to become an initiator—you can't let the interview proceed for too long without getting in your three position points.* Your positive points are your "islands of safety," places you can hop to when asked a question you don't want or one that doesn't fit your game plan.

"Positive" means offer your positive points with positive words, not negative ones. Volunteer information to make a positive point. You have a job to do during the interview: to score with your three positive points. Allow nothing to keep you from your goal. In addition to positive points, you must also have examples, as well. These can be in the form of stories or anecdotes that illustrate your positive points. Stories are what people remember. Try to be an anecdotal interviewee.

During any interview before a camera or microphone, remember to be:

- brief
- emotional
- entertaining
- enthusiastic
- energetic
- positive

In other words, BEEEEP.

Being brief means being able to state each positive point in twenty seconds or less, radio prefers less, talk show and print more. Since television cameras as well as radio tend to "flatten" people—make them seem bland—you have to exhibit at least two of the Es to project an interesting interview and to be remembered by the audience, who are probably distracted while watching and listening to you.

At all times, when giving an interview on television and radio (or with the print media for that matter), you must take charge of the interview so that you optimize how you come across and hence, your marketing impact, because there is no such thing as "off the record," and "the camera never blinks." Don't say anything you don't want to hear broadcast on TV or radio or see in print. Giving background information is fine, and there may be some reporters/hosts/interviewers you can trust. But as a general rule, consider everything you say to be ON the record.

Occasionally, and depending on the subject, you may get hostile or difficult questions. Don't get rattled, or repeat any negative sentences or phrases. Correct misinformation quickly and go on to state a positive point. If you are asked a hypothetical question, you can remind the host that you don't have a crystal ball but you can ask, "Do you know that . . . ?", and state a positive point.

When former Los Angeles Laker Coach Pat Riley was interviewed during halftime of the 1990 NBA Finals, "At the Half" host Pat O'Brien kept asking Riley if he had made the decision to retire from the Lakers. Riley finally addressed it by taking charge of the interview. He eloquently said, "I appreciate your journalistic instincts to get information, but as I stated before, the decision won't be made until next week." O'Brien was floored: end of question, close of interview—as gracefully as possible.

What if you receive several questions in a row? Kalish says pick the one YOU want to answer then ask the interviewer to repeat another question. It's not up to you to remember his questions.

SIT UP AND SCORE

Karen Kalish recommends that you sit with your derriere well back in the chair and lean forward, which gives you an air of authority and credibility. If your back is resting against the back of the chair, you will appear to be too comfortable; sit alert and lean forward. Your hands should be free to gesture, not be glued to the arms of the chair or to each other. Gesturing makes for a more interesting interview and lets off nervous energy.

When the engineer asks for a voice level, state your name, spell your last name, give your title and the subject of the interview. That simple technique communicates a world of information: they get their voice levels, the correct pronunciation and spelling of your last name and your firm. Also, the reason for the interview is made clear to everyone in the vicinity, including the interviewer.

Act as if the microphone is always on. Several years ago, a local talk show ended his show on Friday by saying, "Have a good weekend." Then the audience heard, "That should hold the bastards!" Unfortunately, his mike was still on.

CLOTHES THAT DON'T CLASH

Clothing is important. Blues, grays, khakis and pastels look the best. Kalish says that the uniform for men should be a blue suit or sport coat, pastel shirt, red or burgundy tie. Shoes should be polished and repaired. Socks should be above the calf. Beware a shiny forehead and five-o'clock shadow.

Women should wear a suit or dress with sleeves, no flashy prints or sexy frills, and closed-toe black shoes. Don't wear anything that will possibly distract from what you are saying. No white, black, yellow, green or bright anything, or chunky, shiny, flashy jewelry.

BRIDGES AND HIGHWAYS

How do you get from an answer that doesn't make a positive point to one of your positive points? By using bridges, those phrases that get you from their answer to yours. Use such phrases as:

127

- "It's important to tell your viewers (listeners, readers) . . ."
- "I'm also frequently asked . . ."
- "For instance . . ."
- "You should also know that . . ."
- "That's not my area of expertise, but I do know that . . ."

If you don't know an answer, Kalish advises, say so and promise to get the answer as soon as possible. And do. Even though the viewers won't actually know if you obtained the answer or not your commitment to obtaining the answer to a question will score points for you with the interviewer or the producer, as well as listeners.

AN INTERVIEWEE'S BILL OF RIGHTS

You have many rights where the media is concerned. When a reporter (from either broadcast or print media) calls you for an interview, rather the other way around, there are *ten* questions you should always ask.

What is the topic?

When is the interview?

Where will it be (if you prefer it at your office say so).

How long will it take? (20 to 30 minutes is plenty for radio or TV, print may take a bit longer)

Who will conduct the interviews? (then watch, listen or read something by this person to gain familiarity with their style)

> If on a panel, with whom?
>
> Why you?
>
> Will it be aired live (unedited) or taped?
>
> When will it air?

The more you know, the more prepared you can be, and the better the interview you will offer. When a radio or print reporter calls and wants to do an interview on the phone, get their number and say you'll call them right back. In those few minutes, rehearse your three most positive selling points about the subject you would like to promote, say them out loud, take a deep breath and call back, remembering you said you would get right back to them.

If it's ten seconds before show time and you blank out and forget your entire interview "strategy," at the very least you should smile and be open. You have a glorious opportunity for promotion when being interviewed. Use it.

STAR IN YOUR OWN COMMERCIAL

Increasingly, corporate CEOs, as well as successful entrepreneurs on a local level, star in their own commercials. This can serve as an effective marketing strategy for their companies, and to more fully develop and promote the images of the individuals in question.

For years, Lee Iacocca, chairman of the Chrysler Corporation, in television commercials told us that if we could "find a better built American car, buy it." As head of one of the fifteen largest industrial corporation in America, Iacocca's visibility was, of course, already substantial. Victor Kiam, the man who "bought the company" when he was so impressed by Remington shavers followed suit as did David Mahoney of

Avis, Frank Borman of Eastern Air Lines, and numerous others.

On a local level, the entrepreneur who stars in his own advertisements and backs up the claims with reliable products or services is well on the way to becoming a pillar of the community, and one of its more successful entrepreneurs.

Living in Hartford, Connecticut, in the 1960s meant constant exposure to the television advertisements of Bill Savitz, who billed himself as the "King of Diamonds" and offered P.O.M.G.—Peace of Mind Guaranteed. Savitz Jewelers in downtown Hartford, Connecticut was more than a jewelry store serving the metro area. It was a symbol of happy, healthy entrepreneurship reflected in Bill Savitz's continuing array of advertisements.

Savitz advertised in the local paper, the *Hartford Courant*, on a daily basis. He was active in community, charitable, social, civic and professional associations. He sponsored local television and radio shows, little league teams, fund drives, and was associated with numerous other causes in the Hartford area. In short, he was a one-man positive publicity machine.

Those learning about Savitz for the first time might be tempted to feel that with all these advertisements and exposure he may have been perceived as a relentless pitchman trying to over-sell the public. Not so. Savitz was continually changing his ads, their format, and the particulars, and all the while having fun. His ads changed with the seasons and the times.

At one point he created a jingle which linked some of Hartford's landmarks in such a way that promoted Hartford as well as his own business. His themes were fixed however. Through the years, he remained "the King of Diamonds" offering "P.O.M.G.," and as such maintained one of the most popular, high visibility images the area has ever experienced.

In the Washington, D.C., area, Jhoon L. Rhee a master of self-defense and the martial arts employs many of the same principles as Savitz. Rhee stars in his own ads, and is very active in the Washington charitable and civic scene. His phrase "nobody bothers me" spurred thousands of mothers to send their young sons and daughters to his classes on self-defense.

Rhee's popularity quickly spread throughout the Washington, D.C., area to nine surrounding branch locations. The image of the martial arts master, with his karate black belt and defensive stance, hangs heavy in the minds of those who have been exposed to his ads.

Both Savitz and Rhee, either compelled by burning egos, or simply good business sense, found that starring in their own commercials was a master stroke of public relations, projecting the best of their companies. Why? Because people are basically interested in people. When we buy a diamond from Savitz, or attend one of Rhee's classes, even if we never meet the gentlemen, we still feel as if we gained a little piece of them, thereby enabling us to spend our dollars with more confidence. All things considered, the people who get rewarded in society are those with an image which pleases others.

PROJECTING THE BEST OF YOU

Psychologists have long known that people have been influenced by physical looks, and most of us conclude that what looks good must be good. Personal images are not right or wrong, or good or bad—they are simply the way you come across to other people who come into contact with you. To achieve desired outcomes is a more complicated matter. While no one has the right to tell you how to dress or act, to successfully rise to the top of your field, appearing or acting in certain strategic ways will improve your overall effectiveness. People will usually judge you based on the image that they perceive, and you are always projecting an image whether you are conscious of it or not.

"Falsify or subdue who and what you are," says Don Beveridge in *The Achievement Challenge*, "and your quest for a successful business or for career advancement will short circuit. Those around you will soon see through the facade, distrusting even your honest intentions." Beveridge goes on to say that even if you are successful at projecting something you are not, your own enjoyment will be diminished because of the tremendous energy needed to maintain your invented image.

The trick is to accent the best of you
and minimize the worst.

Find your image niche, which means drawing on the best of what you have to offer. You should observe others, but don't emulate them, unless you want to confuse people. There's enough room in this world for your unique self to come through. If the Richard Simmonses of the world can succeed in show business, then you can make it in business by not imitating those around you. Beveridge says, "Innovate, function, and perform in a way that is consistent with who, what, and where you are as an individual." This does not mean that you should not be constantly learning and picking up things from those around you—especially those who are more experienced than you.

As a means of self-improvement, you may want to hire a wardrobe consultant. Such individuals can be found in the phone book under fashion consultant, image consultant, or wardrobe consultant. The services may vary. Many wardrobe consultants will visit your home, examine your clothes and make specific suggestions to help you project the best of you. For a fee, some will take you shopping, or even shop for you.

If you want to convey the image of being a high-quality professional, doing high-quality work, then think, feel and act quality, within your relationships, regarding your appearance, in the services you provide, and the resources you employ.

After all, the right image is really nothing more than creating positive, trusting assumptions in others.

SITTING ON THE BOARD

"There is no shortage of people who want to get on boards," says Robert K. Mueller, chairman of Arthur D. Little, Inc. Every day, people write to him asking how they can get on boards. There is a strong element of prestige associated with being a board member and particularly of a large well-known corporation, and it is a definite image-booster.

The basic reason PATTs seek to become directors, however, is the ability to exchange ideas with other PATTs. Membership enhances one's visibility and exposure and offers a highly effective marketing shot in the arm. The connections and networking that occur among corporate directors are likely to foster important business and social opportunities that would otherwise not be available.

The typical board of a *Fortune 500* corporation meets nine or ten times a year. Each director spends from 175 to 200 hours per year or nearly five 40-hour weeks serving in this capacity. Directors are paid generally between $24,000 and $33,000 or an hourly rate of about $150. This figure is understandably lower for directors of smaller corporations. For PATTs who are outside directors, tackling the problems and challenges of another corporation helps to strengthen and solidify their power in their own corporations and otherwise accelerate the opportunity to gain marketing insights and multi-organizational experience.

Serving on the board of a large corporation is, in and of itself, a career enhancing strategy for a corporate executive or entrepreneur. Says one observer, "election to the board of a big corporation confers the status unobtainable in ordinary executive and professional life." The entrepreneurial PATT who is also a director greatly benefits from this association in the marketing sense. His company is viewed in an entirely different light because of the first-person connection with the "big boys"—the other members of the corporate board—that the entrepreneur now has.

Mark N. Kaplan, who has been a member of over a dozen boards observes that "boards of directors have a real role to play in ensuring the good health of the business community . . . and advising management on responsibilities to shareholders, customers and employees." In hopes of encouraging more corporations to consider women for their boards, the National Women's Economic Alliance sent out its directory of female directors to the nation's top 1,000 corporations. Pat Harrison, who formed the alliance, seeks to create an organization for high-powered businesswomen who want to obtain more prestige and power. Helping her members to achieve board room appointments is one of the main tenets of her program.

What is the best way to gain board membership? Associate with those who are already directors. Like many things in business, those who get appointed/elected to a board have inside connections.

IMAGE ENHANCEMENT IN THE PROFESSIONS THROUGH CERTIFICATION

On their letterhead and stationery, following the names of PATTs, especially those in the professions, one frequently sees some initials other than those indicating higher education degree. The initials *C.A.E. (Certified Association Executive), C.F.P. (Certified Financial Planner),* and *C.M.A. (Certified Management Consultant)* indicate various types of professional certification. Clients and customers look to certification and licensing as a way of judging the credentials and experience of professionals. It lets us know that the professionals we hire have passed certain examinations or qualifications set by their industry.

Institutionalized License procedures such as *M.D.* tell us that the person has completed the training necessary to meet standards set by law. Dentists have *D.D.S.* after their names, indicating successful completion of training and an examination. Licensing applies to individuals and is granted by a political body to people who meet predetermined qualifications. Licensing is required by law before professionals can engage in certain occupations, such as being a doctor or dentist.

Accreditation is frequently confused with certification and/or licensing. Accreditation applies to programs rather than individuals, generally those of a school, college, institute, or university. It is granted by an association to organizations that meet standards determined through initial and periodic evaluations.

Certification is granted by an association to professionals who meet predetermined qualifications, but it is voluntary. A Certified Public Accountant (C.P.A.) signifies a certification of quality in the profession of accounting. More than 300 associations and societies offer professional certification programs. Here's a sampling of certification titles:

Certified Association Executive
Certified Commercial Investment Member
Certified Financial Planner
Chartered Financial Analyst
Certified Management Consultant
Certified Military Club Manager
Certified Public Accountant
Certified Safety Professional

In many professions, the certification process involves an examination, a written code of ethics that professionals must sign, and a description of the experience the professional must have to warrant certification.

If certification in any field is to signify ability and experience adequately, the process of certification is rigorous. After all, if it were easy to get certified, the certification would soon be worth very little to its recipients and their clients.

Many professionals complain about certification procedures as "jumping through too many hoops," but they know the process of applying and earning acceptance is essential for a professional designation.

The requirements to become a Certified Management Consultant, for example, include five years' experience as a management consultant and at least one as a project manager. The applicant must submit five client engagement summaries, including one client engagement described in detail, plus three client references, and three associate references. In addition, there is a written test, an interview with a panel of three existing Certified Management Consultants, an application fee, an initiation fee and annual dues.

About one-third of the Certified Management Consultants come from large national consulting firms like Kurt Salmon Associates or Booz, Allen and Hamilton. Another third come from major management advisory services (MAS) divisions of large accounting firms such as Ernst & Young, and Deloite & Touche. The rest are from small and one-person firms.

Certification programs offer many image-related benefits for the professional receiving certification including:

Recognition. When you are able to use a designated certification label with your name, people within and outside your industry recognize that you have a certain degree of expertise in your field. Even though they may not know anything about the certification requirements or the certifying association, they automatically regard you as being a cut above the rest.

Networking. Certification provides occasions to become involved with the certifying association, to attend conferences, to speak at meetings, or simply have a common ground for discussions with others who are also certified. Typically, this generates a professional network of colleagues who can refer business to you when they are either too busy or not suited to handle a client.

Keeping Current. Because you are exposed to top professionals in your field, you are encouraged and inspired to keep your knowledge and abilities current, all of which enhances your position in the industry. You may also do this by attending seminars and conferences offered through the certifying association or by reading the magazines and other publications the association may distribute.

Self-Assessment. The process of applying for certification can be a valuable self-assessment and development tool as you prepare for the certifying examination and/or review your achievements in writing for the application. Many certifications require periodic updating which allows you continued opportunities for reassessing your professional strengths and weaknesses.

Even after becoming certified it is still up to you to reap the greatest possible benefits from this achievement. By all means, be sure to take advantage of your certification. Add your newly designated title to your stationery and business cards. Make sure it is included when anything is written about you. Submit articles to publications related to your area of certification. Take a leadership role in organizing and conducting any local meetings of professionals in your field. Get involved and stay involved to let your certification really work for you.

PROJECTING AN IMAGE THAT LASTS

Within your profession or outside of it, perhaps the most effective way to create a positive image that enables others to remember something about you is to become known for something. Among companies, Merrill Lynch positions itself as "a breed apart." Henry Block of H&R Block has "29 reasons" why you should let H&R Block compute your taxes for you. Some accountants develop a reputation for superior tax work while others get known for auditing, and still others specialize in financial planning services.

If you have the talent to develop your own specialized software to or invent a new product, then more power to you. This is the ultimate way of becoming known. If you can't figure out a method to become known for something creative, there are several other ways to make your mark and gain recognition. Some managers are well known because they have become experts at flex-time work programs, others at coaching their employees, and others at highly motivating them. Unusual hobbies (but not too far out) such as cross-country snowmobiling or white water rafting can also be used effectively to stamp one's image in the minds of others.

A common mistake made by too many professionals is trying to be all things to all people, which often leads to being not much to anyone. One up-and-comer, a 26-year-old body builder, is known and kidded about his weight-lifting, throughout the company he works for—all 1,600 people. Now that's visibility. Combined with doing good work it should help to accelerate his progression to the top over others with similar business talents but a less recognizable image.

POWER IMAGES OF PATTS

Whether you like him or not, Donald Trump has the capability to fill up a room the moment he enters it. His personal energy level is enormous. Without being loud or showy, he is a magnet for the attention of others. While some people can be in a room for hours and you don't even notice them, with Trump this is almost impossible.

Because of the breakup with his wife, Ivana, and his lingering financial woes, Trump has recently received more publicity than he cares to. Yet, he remains as one of the world's masters in generating a power image.

When Mikhail Gorbachev visited the United States in 1988, Trump instantly shifted his position while greeting the Soviet leader so that a nearby photographer captured both of them in profile as opposed to one or the other with his back to the camera. The photo made the wire services and was reprinted worldwide, conveying for at least that one image, a sense of equality between the two men.

Speaking of Soviet Leaders, in the 1950s and early 1960s Nikita Khrushchev struck terror in the hearts of Americans at the United Nations by pounding his shoe on the table and saying, "We will bury you." Khrushchev was particularly adept at such tactics whenever the U.N.'s Security Council or General Assembly was facing important issues with implications for Soviet security.

Years later, a journalist who was reviewing old UPI photos discovered that during one of Khrushchev's many infamous shoe-pounding sessions, *both of his shoes were on his feet.* A power player extraordinaire, he was using a third shoe that he apparently brought for the specific purpose of making his hallmark grandstand play.

In concluding this chapter, there are two more looks at the images projected by contemporary people at the top.

Irving R. Levine

CBS News correspondent Levine travels frequently on the shuttle between New York and Washington, D.C. As a newsman it is important for Levine to carefully read the *New York Times* and *Washington Post* on flights. In doing so, he puts on a pair of thin white gloves to absorb the smears that newsprint leaves, which would otherwise go on his hands and ultimately dirty his clothes. The always dapper Levine isn't concerned about what others think of the funny-looking gloves. He wants and needs to read the news, and wants to step off the plane clean and ready for his next appointment.

Sam Walton

The legendary founder and president of Wal-Mart Stores, Walton was reportedly one of the richest men in America. (The Walton family recently divided up the family fortune for tax purposes and now they are one of the richest families in America.) Wal-Mart consistently earns more per square foot

139

than the competing Sears, K Mart, or J.C. Penney Stores. Walton, with a fortune somewhere above $6 billion, constantly receives press coverage in the nation's major newspapers and business magazines.

One of the many secrets to his success is the degree to which he supercharges his troops. Walton is one of the most high-spirited enthusiastic corporate leaders to ever grace the business scene. As with most strong and successful leaders, his words and image heavily impact his employees.

Walton is well known for his warm, down-to-earth approach to retailing, driving around in a humble pickup truck despite his vast wealth, and regularly eating in local fast-food establishments. Each of his stores reflects a genuine, "we are glad to see you," atmosphere. It is as if Sam was greeting you personally. And this warm, personal approach, in part, has helped make Wal-Mart consistently profitable in an industry known for cycles and red ink.

Chapter Six

Hot Tips/Insights

- An effective public relations strategy can swiftly alter our view about anyone and anything. While we may not find this pleasing, projecting the right image is taking on increasing, not decreasing, importance, even as business and society becomes more sophisticated.

- Many people today are forced to take short cuts or quicker routes to decision making and judgment. People who are effective at influencing others, as well as the most successful sales training programs, incorporate trigger features such as friendship, commitment, consensus, authority and obligation in their presentations.

- Personality is the key to successful image building. to project a winning image, be enthusiastic and well-briefed on your subject matter, maintain eye contact, scan the audience, and periodically focus on a friendly face in the crowd.

- Establish rapport with reporters. Answer questions in a straightforward manner and don't be goaded into responding if you are unsure of the correct answer. Emotional displays are usually counterproductive.

- While giving an interview on air or in the press is a good opportunity to get your point across and gain high visibility, you have to be prepared, and that means going into an interview with an agenda.

- Your goal should be to make three positive points in any interview situation. Interviewers will have their own list of questions to ask, but don't assume they will be the "right" questions. Your positive points are your "islands of safety," places you can hop to when asked a question that doesn't fit your game plan.

- During any interview before a camera or microphone, remember to be: brief, emotional, entertaining, enthusiastic, energetic, and positive.

- Increasingly, corporate CEOs, as well as successful entrepreneurs star in their own commercials as an effective marketing strategy for their companies, and to more fully develop and promote their personal images.

- People will usually judge you based on the image that they perceive. You are always projecting an image whether you are conscious of it or not.

- Accent the best of you and minimize the worst. Find your image niche, which means drawing on the best of what you have to offer. Observe others, but don't emulate them, unless you want to confuse people.

- As a means of self-improvement, consider hiring a wardrobe consultant.

- The right image is really nothing more than creating positive, trusting assumptions in others.

- There is a strong element of prestige associated with being a board member, particularly of a large, well-known corporation, and it is a definite image-booster.

- PATTs seek to become directors to exchange ideas with other PATTs. The connections and networking that occur among corporate directors are likely to foster important business and social opportunities that would otherwise not be available.

- Clients and customers look to certification and licensing as a way of judging the credentials and experience of professionals. It lets one know that the professionals we hire have passed certain examinations or qualifications set by their industry.

- Certification programs offer many image-related benefits for the professional receiving certification including recognition, networking, and self-assessment.

- A common mistake made by too many professionals is trying to be all things to all people, which often leads to being not much to anyone.

- One of the most effective ways to create a positive image that enables others to remember something about you is to become known for something.

PART III

MONEY: HAVING IT AND PROTECTING IT

Chapter Seven

THE RICH AND THE VERY RICH

> *Money is not power, control, love or security, dependency or independency, control or self-worth. Money is really, merely money, after all.*
>
> —Olivia Mellan, trainer,
> "Money and Harmony"™

The Beatles said, "Money can't buy you love," but that didn't stop them from getting rich. Even if it can't buy you love, it is probably the most widely used barometer of success in society. The successful find that the raw power of money depends on the ability to continue to get it, invest it and manage it easily.

People with power and protocol who make it to the top of their professions, understandably, are an affluent lot. This chapter and the one that follows takes an insider's look at the rich as a class, then the very rich, for insights as to what they value, problems they incur related to wealth, and strategies they employ to protect their financial resources.

147

Those in top positions are compensated with large sums of money and are obviously an envied segment of society. They tend to drive late model cars, own nice homes, and exude a distinctive and comfortable air of power. A study titled *Success in America,* published by CIGNA, the large life insurance conglomerate, reveals that contrary to some media portrayals, upper-affluent Americans are not necessarily snobby people who squander or ignore the problems of the less-fortunate. Instead, they generally are found to exhibit *high moral and value standards, and are solid members of society.* Many are frequent benefactors of charities and participate in organizations that strengthen their community.

While the potential decline of the family as an institution has been a topic of continuing social debate, among PATTs the vast majority believe in the fundamental importance of family. CIGNA's study indicates that 83% of upper-affluent Americans are married and most have children. This is a strong indication that *among PATTs families may actually take precedence over business-related affairs.*

It is likely that PATTs get to the top due in part to the strength and inspiration of their family life, where personal relationships are very important.

Those having $125,000 in income or a net worth of $600,000, excluding the value of primary residence, are regarded by society as upper-affluent. Younger members of this group, a minority, are seen as more risk-oriented. Older members tend to be more conservative and risk averse. Regardless of age or experience the PATTs seem to share certain traits: optimism, diligence, rationality, and realism.

PATTS: OPTIMISTIC ABOUT SUCCESS

As a group, PATTs believe that their economic situation will continue to be successful or improve. A self-fulfilling upward cycle ensues, and optimism and success are the catalysts for hard work and even more success. They are generally self-made individuals with specific goals who do everything in their means to reach them. One in five say they plan to never retire.

When it comes to financial planning, PATTs tend to be conservative and careful. In this respect they are different from most people in society who use whim or intuition to make important money-related decisions. Most PATTs seek personal financial assistance from CPA's, stockbrokers, attorneys, and financial planners. Surprisingly, women and those under the age of 55 are more likely to seek out personal financial assistance which may be attributed to the notion that men are more "business oriented" than women, and that older individuals are more experienced and capable in their finances.

With investments some take calculated risks and hope for big financial gains, while most want to hold on to solid assets and avoid risks. Men are more likely to be risk-takers than women. The top two investments of upper-affluent households are real-estate and stocks. They are also active investors in money market funds, passbook saving accounts, and life insurance policies, among many others investments. The more risk-oriented invest in high-yield junk bonds and highly leveraged commodity investments.

In households with the main income producer under age 55, the prime investments are real estate and stocks. In households where the chief provider is between 55 and 64, stocks are preferred over real estate and money market funds. In households where the main income producer is 65 or over, money markets take precedence while stocks, bank-issued CDs, and real estate are preferred in that order.

These findings demonstrate one of two things: as one gets older, he gets wiser and handles his money in different, productive ways, or, as one ages, the responsibilities of maintaining real estate investments becomes too burdensome, and hence, other investments become more attractive. It appears as the upper-affluent get older, they want their money in more

149

stable, liquid accounts and in the hands of someone they know such as their banker or personal broker.

BEYOND MONETARY GOALS

PATTs view personal goals as monumentally important. Their interpretation of success includes their family, children's education, and career. They seek to apply their talent, creativity, and energy to its maximum potential and feel to give any less of themselves would cheat or hinder their quest toward success.

The CIGNA study found that a low percentage place a high value on the importance of material goods. For example, only 11 percent feel owning an expensive car is important (though many have expensive cars), and only 11 percent think owning important works of art or antiques is essential. A mere 7 percent felt belonging to a prestigious private club is important. These are interesting findings because society generally views the rich as mainly concerned with their luxurious goods and hollow, high-society lives, a view which is partially attributable to the media's one-sided coverage of the affluent.

The lesson to be learned in studying the upper-affluent is to place a high value on other people. The upper-affluent believe in having someone special to provide for; someone special to rely on; and someone special to trust.

LESSONS FROM THE VERY RICH

From the beginning of history there has always been a fascination with the very rich. From Egyptian mummy King Tut to John D. Rockefeller to Sam Walton, society has always been enamored by their wealth and power. Our perception of wealthy people may lead us to believe that money alone provides their power and prestige. What about the time, however, when many wealthy individuals did not have vast sums of money?

In their ascension toward wealth, did the very rich demonstrate a special skill or capability that enabled them to reach the pinnacle of success? This is an intriguing point because if the "secrets" of the very rich could be revealed, then theoretically we all could become very wealthy by following their advice. Unfortunately, the answer to wealth and success is not simple, so let us examine and analyze the behavior of those who are very rich and at the top.

The very rich are an interesting lot to analyze. Their stories and lives often are inspiring and touching. Some start with nothing and work their way up, while others inherit substantial sums and make them grow to much larger sums. They do not necessarily always exhibit high intelligence or special knowledge, but they do possess a strong belief in themselves which leads to self-confidence and determination.

Externally, the very rich appear no different from others. They are short, tall, fat, skinny, old, and they watch the evening news just like everyone else. The list goes on and on. The similarities, however, end with their unique qualities of leadership, persistence, focus, inspiration, and imagination embodied by the likes of entrepreneurs such as Henry Ross Perot, who is ranked as one of three richest individuals in America, or Jack Kent Cooke, owner of the Washington Redskins. The intangible qualities possessed by the very wealthy are not taught in school, rather, they are rules or habits that were picked up along the way and maintained.

FOLLOWING HIS OWN COUNSEL

Some of the very rich learned their unique qualities and values at a young age. Henry Ross Perot, for example, grew up in the depression era when jobs were scarce; in fact there were so few jobs that working adults would accept any position available regardless of wages. As a child, Perot was smart and

151

innovative. At age 12, he approached the circulation manager of his town newspaper, *The Gazette,* and offered to deliver newspapers to people's homes in the poverty-stricken slum of town. No one had ever conceived of this idea—the prevailing assumption was that poor people could not afford, let alone read a newspaper.

Perot knew otherwise. *An incurable optimist who followed his own counsel, he did not listen to what skeptics said.* He felt that if he worked hard, positive results would follow—and they did. Within a short period Perot was making so much money by delivering newspapers that his commission was in jeopardy of being reduced.

Never one to sit back and let others control his destiny, Perot wrote to the publisher and complained about how he was being treated by the paper's management after making so much money for the paper. The publisher agreed with him and he was able to continue the lucrative arrangement he had set up.

Creativity was a vital component in Perot's success. While working for IBM and becoming their top sales representative (a PATT at an early age), he conceived of initiating a service branch within IBM, which would help client companies learn how to use and apply office technology to improve their business operations. IBM declined to follow through on his idea, and Perot, at age 31, decided to leave his high commission earning job to start his own company.

Perot formed the Texas-based Electronic Data Systems (EDS) and became as close to an overnight success as one can get. The company employed top caliber people who were committed to solving customer problems on time and within budget. All the while Perot restricted himself to a $68,000 salary, while his net worth on paper grew by 1968 to $350 million.

In 1970, disaster struck. The price of the company's stock was being bid up at a feverish rate. Eventually, EDS stock plummeted. In a single day, the company's stock, of which Perot was the major shareholder lost $450 million, the costliest one-day loss in New York Stock Exchange history. Perot's response was one of ambivalence and indifference, citing that money was not the primary goal for his success. (It should be noted that he was easily able to absorb a loss of that magnitude without affecting his lifestyle.)

Characteristically, Perot persevered. The company faced many other challenges along the way, but under Perot's steady leadership enjoyed impressive growth. In 1984, he sold EDS to General Motors for $2.5 billion and in 1986 sold his remaining stock in the company for $700,000,000. In 1988, Perot launched Perot Systems and has ambitious plans for the new computer services firm.

Perot gained hero status in America when he devised and financed a daring rescue mission for several of his employees stranded in Iran as Khomeini came to power. He is also well-remembered for sponsoring and paying for a ticker-tape parade for the returning P.O.W.'s. His status as one of the richest men in America is secure.

HABIT AND PLEASURE

In his book *Power*, Michael Korda notes: "In an age when the Puritan work ethic seems irrelevant, there are primarily four reasons for working: (1) Habit; (2) Pleasure; (3) Money; (4) Power." People who amass ample amounts of money and power are left with only two possible motivations to continue their gainful employment—fortunately habit and pleasure are sufficient to keep most PATTs satisfied.

If the very rich have one thing in common
it is that they find great pleasure in what they do.
With this attitude, there is little wonder
why the very rich keep getting richer.

Though he is 77 years old, Jack Kent Cooke, sports franchise owner and media emperor still works more than ten to eleven hours a day. Cooke is the man who built and owned the Forum in Los Angeles. He also owned the Los Angeles Lakers and Los Angeles Kings (hockey teams). Like Perot, Cooke maintains an uncanny air of optimism, mixed with persistence.

Cooke has no intentions of retiring. Following a severe heart attack in 1973, Cooke mused: "I am resentful of the fact that a thing like a coronary thrombosis would have the audacity to stop me from doing what I want to do." Characteristic of Cooke's will and determination, only his passing will interrupt his work.

Because the very rich can do whatever they desire when it comes to working, the money naturally becomes secondary. Money is no longer an impetus for success and becomes just a bonus.

Take the example of young billionaire William Gates III. He was a self-taught computer programmer at 13, and by 19, the founder of Microsoft. In 1979, Gates had an extraordinary vision of putting a personal computer on every desk and in every home, and to this day he is a leader in making this dream a reality. Money has never been his focus—it's achievement. The still-single superstar of the software world is known to occasionally work at the office until midnight.

Warren Buffet, the innovative head of Berkshire Hathaway and Buffet Foundation, continues to work eight to ten hour days despite his $3.6 billions in assets. Buffet says that he is simply doing what he wants to be doing and has been since age 20. He also claims to do only deals with people he likes.

As with any PATT, the very rich put money aside in various investments and bank accounts for reasons of prudence and protection. With their primary investment concerns taken care of, the very rich are free to pursue high-risk endeavors or charitable causes with fewer worries.

INNOVATION, IMAGINATION, AND INITIATIVE

Most of the very rich possess innovation and imagination. Ed Bass, an environmentalist, has developed a $30 million artificial ecosystem known as Biosphere II. The 2½ acre project, which includes a mini-rain forest, desert, and ocean, is all under glass, and will provide new findings on humankind's ability to adapt to other environments, though Bass' major quest is to see if the ecosystem can become self-sustaining.

Experiments such as Bass' initially are often met with scorn and skepticism. Yet, those who become very rich often are the ones who ignore the naysayers and look beyond today. They ask themselves, "What will be needed in 5, 10, or 20 years?"

The very rich also exhibit a high level of initiative. They rarely sit back and assume things will take care of themselves, instead they exercise the ability to make things happen. With initiative comes risk, success and failure. The very rich often start as undercapitalized entrepreneurs who believe dreams are meant to be executed while realizing they will not always be successful.

Consider Kavelle R. Bajaj, who came to the United States from India in 1974 and faced more than just business risks—she also suffered through cultural and gender barriers. In her conservative Indian upbringing, Bajaj was expected to place family affairs over a career. Nevertheless she opened a small business selling imported goods, but almost immediately became dissatisfied and disappointed in this venture.

Eventually she opted to try again. In the early 1980s following the breakup of American Telephone and Telegraph, Bajaj saw another business opportunity. She borrowed $5,000 and took computer and database management classes at a nearby college, then started a company called I-Net which provides telecommunication contracting services primarily to the Department of Defense.

The company developed a solid reputation and grew quickly, if not evenly over the next several years. In 1990,

Bajaj landed a $100,000,000 long-term contract from the Air Force for computer systems engineering and software. In all, the company now has 11 offices and 300 employees nationwide, and anticipates growing to 1,000 employees. Bajaj attributes her success to initiative and commitment to ideals. "There is opportunity in the United States for the person who wants to make it," she says. "There is no reason to make excuses."

THE PERILS OF BEING TOO SUCCESSFUL

H. L. Mencken once said, "For every problem, there is a solution which is simple, neat and wrong." Although few rich and very rich would actually opt to trade their riches for rags, most admit that their situations do include a down side. If you only want insights on getting to the top and prefer to deal with the new problems after you've arrived, you might want to skip this cautionary section entirely.

Unwanted publicity for those at the top is a frequent complaint, especially when it is erroneous or unduly personal. Family problems are fairly common for all of us, but sometimes they are even worse for the very rich. To have one's personal and financial affairs scrutinized by the media because of success at work occasionally is part of the baggage that comes along with being very successful.

> *Could you imagine having to deal with your*
> *personal or financial affairs being regularly*
> *discussed in the media? This is often*
> *the case for those at the top, in highly visible*
> *and successful positions.*

In addition to the public scrutiny brought on being at the top, the rich *can suffer psychological tensions that are very different from the ones experienced by the masses.* The special anxieties of the successful and powerful and of their family members commonly fall into three categories: guilt, self-doubt and isolation.

Some agonize over the possibility of losing everything; others worry that they're not worthy of the pinnacle they've reached; still others fret that the rest of the world only sees their achievements or wealth, not the "real" person.

HOW PATTS HANDLE THE DOWNSIDE OF SUCCESS

All manner of dealing with the difficulties of outrageous success have been attempted over the years. The management strategies generally boil down to one of the following:

- learn to live with it
- dodge it
- divest it
- protect it

Learning to Live with It. A new specialty has developed among psychologists who help the very successful make do with what they've got.

Dodging It. This a trait primarily of those who inherited their wealth, not earned it.

Divesting It. There is always the possibility of simply getting rid of the money, and in doing so, getting rid of the afflictions of "affluenza."

Protecting It. Protecting lifetime earnings can be a full time endeavor and nearly is for many (see next chapter on banking relationships). Obviously, there are investments to protect against inflation and trusts to shelter funds. Another type of protection stems from the desire of PATTs to determine exactly who gets their hands on the fortune when it passes from one set of hands to others. The most frequent causes for concern in this regard are death and divorce. Determining how the money will be treated on these occasions is a difficult, family-wrenching task.

Although the proceeds of most fortunes still pass on to spouses and children, there is a growing trend toward managing money by denying it to children. While some of this trend results from the many parents who disinherit sons and daughters in anger, many parents simply don't think their children need the money. They have raised the kids, educated them, and helped them in many other ways. Any more might not be in the kids' best interest; and friends and charitable organizations may need the money more.

One multi-millionaire technology entrepreneur plans for only small sums of his money to go to his children. He has paid to educate them and given them "nominal sums" upon graduation from college, and considers that to be enough help with life. He intends the bulk of his estate to go to charities, after providing adequate security for his wife.

Another problem in protecting one's lifetime earnings is due to the nature and frequency of divorce settlements. It is certainly a blow for those with accumulated wealth to see it walk out the door with a departing spouse—be it the male or female. Divorce law has become precarious to the point where following death, taxes and spendthrift heirs, divorce has become a major natural enemy of wealth. In community property states there is wide latitude about what is and isn't marital property. And so, prenuptial and even postnuptial agreements have become very popular among marriage-minded PATTs.

Now let's turn to pro-active strategies for protecting wealth through the development of banking relationships.

Chapter Seven

Hot Tips/Insights

- Upper-affluent Americans tend to exhibit *high moral and value standards, and are solid members of society.* Many are frequent benefactors of charities and participate in organizations that strengthen their community.

- Among PATTs, families may actually take precedence over business-related affairs, and many PATTs get to the top due in part to the strength and inspiration of their family life, where personal relationships are very important.

- PATTs to share certain traits: optimism, diligence, rationality, and realism. They believe that their economic situation will continue to be successful or improve and a self-fulfilling upward cycle ensues.

- They are generally self-made individuals with specific goals who do everything in their means to reach them.

- When it comes to financial planning PATTs tend to be conservative and careful. One in five say they plan to never retire.

- With investments some take calculated risks and hope for big financial gains, while most want to hold on to solid assets and avoid risks. Men are more likely to be risk-takers than women.

- PATTs view personal goals as monumentally important. Their interpretation of success includes their family, children's education, and career. They seek to apply their talent, creativity, and energy to its maximum potential and feel to give any less of themselves would cheat or hinder their quest toward success.

- The lesson to be learned in studying the upper-affluent is to place a high value on other people.

- The answer to wealth and success is not simple; in the world of business, the very rich do not demonstrate superior skills or special capabilities that enable them to succeed over the average entrepreneur.

- The very rich *do* possess strong belief in themselves which leads to self-confidence and determination, though externally, they appear no different from others.

- Many of the very wealthy, like H. Ross Perot, are incurable optimists who follow their own counsel and do not listen to what skeptics say.

Chapter Eight

POWER BANKING

Cash is virtue.

—Lord Byron

Many PATTs have discovered that a strong relationship with a banker can be crucial for maintaining wealth. That relationship often starts with cultivating one's local banker and ends at the top of the banking pyramid—private banking. Let's invert the discussion so as to begin with the more alluring world of private banking.

PRIVATE BANKING

Probably the ultimate in banking services for individuals is what is called private banking—basically a direct one-to-one, preferred relationship between the banker and you. The concept of offering private banking services, also known as preferred or custom services, is no secret to the very rich. Bankers haven't gone out of their way, however, to share it with their less affluent customers.

One can trace the roots of private banking to the Middle Ages, when bankers, freed from the Church's previous injunctions against charging interest on money, quickly began to cater to the powerful or rich with special care. To pay for enterprises like the Hundred Years War, just as the military ties of medieval feudalism were breaking down, kings had no choice but to borrow money.

The various great banking houses of the Renaissance—the Medici and the Fuggers—became key political players because of close relationships with their customers in the royal houses dominating the rising nation-states of Europe. With the rise of international trade, private banking in its modern form has flourished in Europe since 1672. English, as well as Swiss, French, and German bankers all provided special services to their upper-crust customers.

American banks, especially in old money cities like New York, Boston and San Francisco, have established their own traditions of service and attention on this side of the Atlantic. The decorum and ambience can be something to behold. The favored patrons of Manufacturers Hanover with net worth in excess of $1 million, are gently guided into lavish private offices with deep pile carpeting and elegantly wood-panelled walls.

No fewer than two officers well-acquainted with the customer's finances will be prepared to meet the his requests. Here, one can obtain medium- to high-six-figure mortgage loans, often with no more difficulty than that of an average customer when using an automatic teller machine. "Manny Hanny" will also arrange complimentary lunches for you in its private dining room to discuss stock market transactions, long-term investment programs, or line-of-credit arrangements among a host of other financial topics.

The Perks of Power

You want service? One time, a preferred customer of New York's Chase Manhattan Bank found he needed to make a large withdrawal after the bank had closed on the day before a national holiday. No problem. The bank delivered the check to the customer's apartment on the morning of the holiday. Often, service at this level does not take a holiday.

For culture vultures, U.S. Trust may be worth one's patronage. The bank has been known to offer private lectures on diverse investment subjects such as precious metals, fine wines, and oriental rugs.

COMING TO A BANK NEAR YOU

New York isn't the only place where money lives, so neither is it the only place to find the perks of private banking. First National Bank of Palm Beach will warehouse customer's furs, as well as precious metals, paintings, and family heirlooms. Six-figure depositors with Houston's Medical Center Bank have been allowed to borrow the bank's airplane, so long as they refill the tank when they're finished.

Bank of America will pamper customers, coast to coast. They will arrange private, high-powered networking in New York for customers. For art lovers, the bank can provide appraisers from Sotheby's and invitations to attend private collection previews before scheduled auctions. Three thousand miles and three time zones west in Beverly Hills, "B of A" caters to clients in sophisticated, Californian style—a plush, private banking lounge, behind a door labeled only by an undistinguished room number.

Allowed by Law

Put in perspective, when it comes to financial services private bankers can provide almost anything allowed by law. The list of services can include personal stock brokerage, assistance with real estate purchases, establishing money market accounts, arranging currency swaps, or intermediary intervention for large business deals.

At New York's Citibank, customers earmarked as special receive a patient, sympathetic ear and expedited completions on their loan requests, enjoying an efficient, flexible red tape bypass. Chemical Bank offers financial services to meet the "life cycle" of the affluent customer. This involves trust services, loans and deposit services and investment management and counseling—fundamental requirements among the targeted groups, needed at different times.

Chase offers qualifying clients—with annual incomes of at least $300,000 or assets totaling the same—similar speedy turnaround on loan applications, lower rates on larger lines of credit, and personalized consulting in investment advice. Beyond expedited service, Chase can give you a full range of financial services. They can restructure your estate, review your will, and inventory your personal assets and liabilities. They can take this information to create a strategy to meet both your short- and long-term financial goals.

NICHE MARKETING

Many private banking units will try to appeal to you by offering the diversity of services and strength of lending resources provided by large institutions while maintaining a personalized, individualized approach. Recently, the American Bankers Association (ABA) in Washington, D.C., indicated that the vast majority of its members now have some type of strategic plan to attract and cater to the affluent customer.

While some might think all this attention to top-dollar customers is just elitism, it is also good business for the bank. Banks and financial institutions traditionally generate most of their revenues on the most affluent 20 percent of their customers, because these depositors, as one industry observer noted, "engage in the highest value transactions." And the upper 20 percent of that most affluent 20 percent represent the Holy Grail to the private banker who is ready to meet their special needs.

More Millionaires

In the marketplace, the number of millionaires in the United States has risen dramatically in the last ten years and now exceeds 500,000. The last decade's entrepreneurial boom encompassing all ages, and several million female entrepreneurs, provided a healthy, visible pipeline of prospects for private banking services. Add foreign investors and the market potential is clear.

This changing market has led some banks to pay more attention than ever to the banking elite. Years ago, Houston's Medical Center Bank restructured itself to attract only doctors and other affluent customers. "You can't be all things to all people," mused its founder, "but I can be all things to the people I select." The bank charged $30 for a bounced check to discourage non-affluent customers from doing business with them.

BANKING FOR THE UP-AND-COMING

Of course, the *sine qua non* of fancy private banking services is having a large source of income or capital reserves. To quote an old adage, it takes money to make money. That means that one needs to have a source of money before investing in projects or ventures that will yield them even more money.

It's not difficult to develop these relationships, PATTs do it all the time. The key is cultivating a retail banker. *Money* magazine conducted a random survey of bankers around the country a few years back, and *all responded that the most important financial move a customer can make is to establish a working relationship with a banker.*

On the road to the top, you may not have the financial clout to rank the special treatment of true personal banking, however, future PATTs get started by what is now called "relationship banking."

With the tightening banking market, many smaller bankers have the same idea in reverse —they are looking for the big customers of the future, and are banking on loyalty early on to carry over to a lucrative future.

This sort of reciprocity has worked for many PATTs when they were starting out. Almost without exception, the whiz kids of the microcomputer industry cultivated bankers to finance their explosive growth. Only after they had established a market presence did they move into the stock market for additional capital.

One bank looking for the next garage-born billionaire is Signet Bank headquartered in Northern Virginia. Signet will assist customers with estate planning and estate accounts, providing custodial services (i.e., tracking the time-consuming details of customers investments and providing regular reports and tax summaries) and setting up living and testamentary trusts, as well as handling a variety of life insurance programs, line of credit programs, and retirement plans.

Signet will also serve as register and transfer agent or exchange agent for corporate security transactions and will serve as trust depository—including buying, selling, receiving, and delivering securities—for its very select customers. The bank will even provide collection services.

Fifth 3rd Bank in Cincinnati provides preferred customers with a direct-dial phone number to a single contact person who is intimately familiar with the caller's account. Then, for the life of the account, you need know and call only one phone number and talk to only one person to conduct your business with the bank—at least while the same banker stays put.

The contact person keeps his customers up to date on new products and services, and variations in rates. He actively relays information he knows or believes the customer will be interested in receiving. "It's nice when you are personally familiar with your bankers," says one officer. "Our approach is to make the customer feel comfortable talking to the account manager, not emphasizing products."

Remote Personal Banking

Closing retail branches doesn't have much effect on private banking customers. As with regular retail banking, you will establish private banking services face-to-face. Thereafter, you can often use mail, telephones, fax machines, or wire services for your transactions. Obviously this yields a substantial time savings.

"Pretty much everything we do can be handled by a telephone call," says one officer with Fifth 3rd Bank in Cincinnati. "We complete car and mortgage loans, and even lines of credit by mail and phone."

Nurturing a Banking Relationship

Here's the anatomy of a successful, growing banking relationship between the president of a title insurance company and her local banker. She started with personal accounts and with help in financing the company's operations. The loans were used to secure properties which offered returns over several years. She also patronized the bank for other services—checking, personal loans, a discount brokerage stock portfolio, and credit cards.

Later, the bank extended her a $60,000 line of credit which she then took to support a $150,000 loan from a larger bank. That loan let her and a partner buy out the title company's owners. After she took control of the title company, its annual revenues increased by 15 percent, topping $1 million after three years. A large part of the bank's staff was invited to, and appeared at, an open house after the company moved. Their comfort in working together was further solidified by mixing the social with the business relationship.

BUNDLED BANKING

Bankers are making it easier to establish a strong banking relationship with them through bundled or packaged banking. With banking packages, you can combine their everyday checking accounts, loans, other lines of credit, and certificates of deposit. As customers decry fees imposed on most individual accounts—per check fees, transaction fees, fees for generating quarterly statements, bundles have become increasingly popular with banks.

Bundling comes without a lot of fees, as banks attempt to lure loyal customers who will deposit most of their nest-eggs in one place—theirs. Most banks require a few thousand dollars in total deposits, a relatively small price to pay for an entree that later can be parlayed into capital.

One government worker established a loyal banking relationship and later was able to get the money she needed for real estate investments. Another woman started with a checking account at Manufacturers Hanover because it was close to her job. She soon found herself going to the bank to handle the money for a side business. Over the years, she was able to finance law school, an investment property, and a summer house.

Twenty years later, she remains with the bank even after becoming a city commissioner. Her accounts have grown from the original checking to include a money market account, an IRA, and a high-yield certificate of deposit.

FEW FRILLS ON THE LOW END

Most general retail bankers service many customers—if you share your banker with fewer than 100 others, you are doing well. If you are like many customers who go on to becoming preferred clients you'll look with some suspicion upon lavish decor and fancy fixtures. Bankers say that most emerging, affluent customers are more interested in service. They are probably time-pressed and more interested in a bank that is responsive, reliable and fast.

Said one banking officer, "All of our new customers have told us they left their previous bank seeking far greater personalized service. Many customers are offended by offices that are too plush, leaving them with a feeling of, 'Am I paying too much?' if a bank's decor is overly opulent."

Anticipatory Banking

Instead of the frills, power players-to-be prefer long-term service. To accommodate this potential high-end customer base, some banks have started what could be called no-frills, anticipatory banking. "You look at the individual and consider his goals and what is he trying to accomplish. Only after receiving that feedback do we tell him what we think we can do for him," says one no-frills banker.

Anticipatory banking expressly does not offer the litany of products and services—like picture checks or free safe deposit boxes—that are available. If you are married, anticipatory banks will treat you and your spouse as a team, since you both tend to be involved in the management of their finances.

Some banks, even at the no-frills level, assign two people to each account—a lending specialist and a deposit placement specialist. The rationale is that the financial environment has become too sophisticated and too complicated for any one banking officer to master it all. If you don't have a bedrock foundation of capital reserves or a fluctuating income, a line-of-credit arrangement might be suggested.

169

Many no-frills customers, while high-income earners, have uneven cash flows and they may want or need to make purchases that are at odds with their incoming cash. Responsive banks strive to take care of all these concerns up front. Among banks practicing an anticipatory approach to providing services, officers and account managers may actively examine account portfolios and attempt to diagnose and project what the customer may need even before the customer himself may recognize it or even know about it.

WHERE THE BANKS ARE

How do you find banks in your area that offer long term banking relationships with special services? Go shopping. Any city with a metropolitan population of 200,000 or more will provide you with a wide variety of banking institutions to consider without venturing far from home.

All of the information you need to start
a short list of banks can be obtained over the phone
and supported by brochures received in the mail.

After that, meet with the bankers. Ask your questions and see how responsive they are and how comfortable you are with them. Banking is business, but a good fit of personalities between you and your banker can make it easier. Banks which are truly customer-oriented and which have developed comprehensive, private banking services for middle-income earners are only to happy to let you know about it.

Conversely, you can tell in matter of minutes when you're dealing with an unresponsive, non-consumer-oriented bank if you can't reach a person of authority easily by phone. If your call is met with lukewarm interest or the bankers aren't available to discuss their offerings, you should probably find another bank that is more anxious for your business—whatever size it may be.

Even after you've found a banker with whom you can build a relationship, you can't be complacent. Also, consider lining up a second banker to have in reserve, in case your existing one becomes unresponsive. As almost any PATT can tell you, that's what a market economy is all about—*banks are not doing you a favor by taking your business.*

LEARNING THE INS AND OUTS

When you start out in a career or a business, if you are like most people, you probably won't have a personal banker or even a favored retail banker that you can approach for a loan. You may need a bank in a new location or perhaps you've outgrown your retail bank for a particularly large project. The recurring paradox is, of course, that right before your great idea is about to succeed is when you most need a reliable banking relationship for additional capital.

It is your very lack of capital, however, that keeps you out of the big leagues. In those instances, knowing some of the ins and outs of getting your foot through the bank's door can mean the difference between getting the money you need on a timely basis and dropping the project.

Edward Mrkvicka, Jr., the former Chief Executive Officer of the First National Bank, headquartered in Marengo, Illinois, and author of *The Bank Book: How to Revoke Your Bank's License to Steal*, paints a hostile picture of bankers, calling them your financial enemies. While this may be too stark a picture, especially if you are dealing with a familiar banker, his suggestions offer a great insight into how to get the money you need, at the lowest cost, just like a preferred customer.

While banks are as eager as ever to loan money to generate interest income, Mrkvicka explains, "they are sometimes so bureaucracy-bound they might choose not to loan money rather than make a risky decision or violate their official internal lending guidelines. When they examine a loan

171

application, bankers often follow a specific set of criteria in deciding whether you are worth their risk."

The strongest black marks are bankruptcies, collections, or court claims—because these indicate that a lender might have a hard time getting repaid. Find out which credit bureau your bank will use to get a report on you. Request your own copy so you know what the banker is using. Then, if the report includes something you dispute, you can challenge it before a final decision is made and it is too late.

If you have a weak spot in the credit report that is inaccurate you can at least explain your side of the story. "Being candid with a loan officer can only help," Mrkvicka said. Otherwise, you might not even be aware of an item in the report that could cost you the loan.

Demonstrating stability in your location and firm, as well as educational attainment are to your advantage in seeking a loan. The strongest argument for lending money for a project, however, is having a good project.

DON'T BE "ALONE" WHEN APPLYING FOR A LOAN

It always helps to get others, such as your lawyer, accountant, or friends who are familiar with a particular bank, to recommend you. You should also include pertinent agreements with partners, preorder arrangements and other documents indicating that the project is actually highly likely to begin and to succeed. The underlying message that you want to present is that you are serious, solid, and know what you are doing. Credibility is everything.

The Financial Statement

An important part of any loan application is the financial statement. This is where you convince the banker that you are worth the risk. Include the assets you can provide as collateral. In establishing the value of your assets, don't inflate them, but do be sure to give yourself the benefit of any doubt. Many banks are likely to downgrade the value of your collateral by as much as a third to protect themselves and limit their exposure, in the event liquidation becomes necessary.

When it comes to actually negotiating the loan, start by whittling away at the extra fees. "Nonrefundable application fees, filing charges and credit check expenses should be covered under the bank's overhead that is paid by interest," Mrkvicka says. You may also be able to reduce the interest rate by pledging stable collateral like stock or a certificate of deposit.

Doing some basic market research can be key to bringing down your interest rate. "There are few threats as effective as taking your business elsewhere," says Mrkvicka, "especially if you have a name and rate that you can quote from elsewhere." But that's only the start of the fees, he warns.

Sticky Fees

If at all possible, try to avoid loan insurance. It can cost you up to 10 percent of the principal and only serves to ensure that the lender gets paid if you die or become disabled. In most cases, banks get a 40 percent commission from insurance carriers on policies that they sell in connection with loans. "If the bank is adamant about being insured, you probably can do better by just taking out a term life insurance policy from your own agent," says Mrkvicka.

*Above all, be prepared to argue every line
item in the application to cut your cost.
You have nothing to lose.*

LOOKING TO THE FUTURE

While banks have changed some of their time-honored traditions with the relaxed regulation of the 1980s, even larger changes are on the horizon that you might be able to exploit. Probably the biggest is the impending demise of the 50-year-old Glass-Steagall Act, which kept banks out of the brokerage business after the Stock Market Crash of 1929.

Already brokerages and banks are buying one another up in anticipation that they soon will be able to provide one-stop shopping for financial services—the ultimate in a bundled account. You may also find yourself dealing with a foreign banker, at least on large projects. None of the 20 largest banks in the world are American; they are all Japanese or European owned.

The Japanese have taken a leading role in funding the building of the downtown Los Angeles skyline; L.A. now surpasses San Francisco in the dollar volume of annual Japanese banking business.

With the consolidation of Europe in 1992, if your project involves investments in Europe, you may also need to be careful in picking a primary banker who already has established roots there. Domestic banks' entry into Europe after 1992 is uncertain.

Closing Advice

Pick a bank that will not only meet your needs now, but can stay with you and satisfy them later. Ask your friends and advisors for recommendations as to which banks have been good and which ones to avoid. Last and most important, the time to establish a rock solid banking relationship, is before you *need* to.

Chapter Eight

Hot Tips/Insights

- A strong relationship with a banker is generally crucial for maintaining wealth.

- The ultimate in banking services for individuals is called private banking, basically a direct one-to-one, preferred relationship between the banker and you. This no secret to the very rich, but bankers haven't gone out of their way to share it with their lesser customers.

- Some banks entertain their private banking customers to discuss stock market transactions, long term investment programs, or line of credit arrangements, among other financial topics.

- When it comes to financial services, private bankers can provide a wide range of services, including personal stock brokerage, assistance with real estate purchases, establishing money market accounts, arranging currency swaps, or intermediary intervention for large business deals.

- Private banking is good business for banks and financial institutions that traditionally generate most of their revenues from the most affluent 20 percent of their customers.

- PATTs continually develop relationships with those who can fund their ventures—it is true that it takes money to make money.

- The most important financial move a future PATT can make is to establish a working relationship with a banker.

- Through bundled or packaged banking, bankers are making it easier to establish a strong banking relationship.

- With banking packages, one can combine their everyday checking accounts, loans, other lines of credit and certificates of deposit.

- Many future PATTs prefer long-term service to frills. To accommodate this potential high-end customer base, some bank have started what could be called no frills, anticipatory banking where each customer's financial goals are considered.

- To find banks in your area that offer long-term banking relationships with special services, first shop around. Any city with a metropolitan population of 200,000 or more will provide you with a wide variety of banking institutions to consider.

- All of the information you need to start a short list of banks can be obtained over the phone and supported by brochures received in the mail.

- After that, meet with the bankers. Ask your questions and see how responsive they are and how comfortable you are with them. Banks that are truly customer-oriented and offer private banking services for middle-income earners will let you know about it.

- When approaching a banker for the first time, particularly when seeking a loan, the underlying message that you want to present is that you are serious, solid and know what you are doing. Credibility is everything.

- Don't apply for a loan on your own—if possible, have others recommend you.

- The time to establish a rock solid banking relationship, is before you *need* to.

PART IV

THE FEMALE CLIMB TO THE TOP

Chapter Nine

WOMEN AT THE TOP IN THE *FORTUNE 500*

> *Self-conquest is the greatest of victories.*
>
> —Plato

Between 1980 and 1988, there was a 260 percent increase in the number of female officers (vice president and above) in *Fortune 500* or *Fortune Service* companies. At the same time, within corporations the number of women holding one of the top five jobs has tripled. Linda Wachner's success at Warnaco —she is one of three female CEOs of *Fortune 500* firms— illustrates the phenomenon of Corporate Women At The Top (CWATTs). Regardless of a person's gender, in the corporate world the focus is on achieving bottom-line results.

For those a rung or two from CEO, the focus is to make it to CEO while running profitable companies. Today, hundreds of women are prepping for corporate officer positions. A few rungs below is a log jam; thousands of women are competing on that level to become senior executives.

Approximately 39 percent of corporate managers today are women, and for the most part, young women. Ten years ago it was closer to 24 percent. A decade ago, 12 percent of business school graduates were women; today it is 42 percent. Hundreds of thousands of women in their late 20s and 30s in the middle-management ranks are eager to move up. Many are controllers or corporate planners who seek career advancement using the same tools as their forerunners: finding a mentor, offering proven results, networking through business organizations and taking advantage of relationships and contacts made along the way.

Edie Fraser, President of the Public Affairs Group in Washington, D.C., surveyed 50 top females in the corporate ranks (and 50 more top female entrepreneurs—the focus of Chapter Ten). Fraser found that women at the top in the corporate world demonstrate an amazing capability to be consistent performers.

With unrelenting fervor, corporate women at the top
rack up accomplishments knowing that a solid
track record is undeniable and required
for the journey they've chosen.

CWATTs are enthusiastic about their progress and proud of their status—reflected in their senior positions, substantial salaries, bonuses and stock options. Whereas many people readily recognize the names of entrepreneurial females who have sought and gained substantial media attention, such as Estee Lauder, Debbi Fields and Mary Kay Ash, female corporate executives are rapidly and quietly moving forward, not flaunting their success with the media.

CASE IN POINT: MYLLE BELL

Mylle Bell is Director of Corporate Planning for BellSouth. An executive search firm retained by the chief executives of BellSouth recruited her from General Electric, where she worked with CEO Jack Welch. Possessing extraordinary planning ability, Bell is devoted to her career. John Clendenin, CEO of BellSouth, is highly supportive of her.

After graduating from Emory University in Atlanta, Bell taught gifted children for one year, she planned to get her doctorate in psychology. However, she met some people with General Electric, her former husband's employer, and accepted a job offer from the company. The couple transferred to Erie, Pennsylvania, where, at age 23, Bell started in information systems.

Initially, Bell had no knowledge of programming computers, but once she learned how, it confirmed her belief that she could learn whatever she needed. Growing from systems development and technology in 1972, she started building her way to the top of middle management.

Bell turned down her first raise because it *did not come with a promotion. When her boss got a check back for the amount of the raise, he was flabbergasted.* He asked her to be patient and returned in a few hours with a big promotion—four levels up, with greater management responsibility—and an even larger raise.

Bolstered by the recognition, she worked diligently to help GE's Locomotive Division move from a 12 percent to a 70 percent market share. "The key was turning the business around and bringing sound management techniques into play, then coordinating the system to achieve financial results," she says. "The process is important; you want to decrease cycle time and increase management's propensity to accept innovation."

Bell then became involved with GE's Consulting Group and moved to GE corporate headquarters. Acknowledged as a fast tracker, she was strategically moved to key management positions within each division, while maintaining activities with the outside consultants. Soon Bell was given responsibility for 21 GE plants globally and for managing GE's half-billion dollar circuit breakers division. She then headed GE's factory automation team.

At all stages Bell used her training in psychology to build strong teams and a strong personal network. All the while, out of necessity, Bell's mentors were men.

Bell was afforded an unprecedented opportunity when BellSouth chairman, John Clendenin, recruited her through an executive recruiter. Happy with her progress at GE, she sat on the offer for several months. However, she had a strong feeling that the move would be a good one, and took the offer. She has since been satisfied with her decision and her progress at BellSouth.

"I think the key to success and happiness on the job is having the commitment to move forward, the desire and excitement to keep learning, and the political skills to coexist in a fast-paced environment," she says.

Today Bell sees higher education as an important tool for reaching the top, but she feels a graduate degree is not mandatory if one has other strengths, such as a tremendous commitment to succeed. She points out three essentials to success:

- the skill to convert information into insight
- the ability to communicate
- the capacity to manage people

"In the corporate world," she says, "being a woman isn't of consequence. The chips on the shoulders [of male executives] are falling down! It's now pure capability that counts." This observation is echoed by other CWATTs.

OPENING DOORS

After years of not being allowed to ascend to top corporate positions, in most major companies female corporate executives today have an open door, with many companies actively grooming their best and brightest. Edie Fraser found that most CWATTs have obtained M.B.A.s. They were recruited right off the business school campuses and are employed by *Fortune 500* companies in the New York, New Jersey, and Connecticut area.

Once, IBM stood alone as the major corporation that promoted women as far up as their ambition would take them. Of late, IBM has been joined by Monsanto, ARCO, General Motors and a host of other companies interested in employing talented, hard-working individuals, regardless of their sex.

On the East Coast, corporate leaders in companies such as IBM, American Express, Corning Glass, Merck, Kodak, and Pitney Bowes—most located along the New York/Connecticut corridor—are providing fertile ground for female career ascent. In newspaper publishing, long a male bastion, Gannett employs six women in executive vice president positions and a dozen other women as publishers of its various newspapers. These companies proudly cite examples of female executives who are progressing up their corporate ladders.

In the Midwest, Sara Lee, General Motors, General Mills, Quaker Oats, Dayton Hudson and Monsanto lead the charge. In the West, leading employers of women include Levi Strauss, ARCO, Mattel and Intel. The South has been slowest with the exception of Federal Express and RJR Nabisco (the latter recently moving its headquarters to New York).

DELIBERATENESS AND ASTUTENESS

Fraser's survey of CWATTs uncovered the lessons they've learned and thus they have advice to offer other aspiring female corporate executives.

> Go to a leading business school.
>
> Join a progressive company in a line job position.
>
> Demonstrate results every step of the way.
>
> Gain support from senior male mentors.
>
> Stay on the upward career track.

Are you deliberate in the way you present yourself to the world? *CWATTs dress, speak, and present ideas with precision.* They take risks—calculated risks with the options weighed and alternatives studied. CWATTs are extremely astute political animals, presenting strategy and rationale in brilliant detail. Everything is documented—the i's are dotted and t's are crossed—and their organizational skills are superb. They watch and weigh each move on the corporate chessboard, planning each step of the way, whether it is meeting a job's responsibilities or making the next career move. Many possess strong financial and marketing backgrounds; each has a solid relationship with a male mentor—often the chief executive officer (CEO) of the corporation.

THE SUPPORT OF A STRONG MALE MENTOR

Successful women were once more threatening to men than they are today. Times have changed. Most men now enthusiastically support and appreciate working with female executives, who in turn recognized early on the importance of finding a strong male mentor. Fraser's research confirms that *one of the smartest moves a rising female star can make is to attract a strong mentor and develop a healthy, long-term professional relationship.*

While their own expectations of their abilities are high, the expectations of CWATTs by their mentors and those around them are just as high. Ask any of the CEOs of a female corporate executive what they expect of her, and you likely will receive a five-minute discourse on her position. Many CWATTs benefit from carefully orchestrated career tracks laid out for them expressly so that they will gain the right types of rigorous experience in their progression to the top; their mentors play an active role in this progression.

Ilene Jacobs's mentor is Ken H. Olsen, President and CEO of Digital Corporation, and a highly respected visionary. Jacobs is vice president and treasurer of Digital's Network Computer Systems. She has been treasurer for five years, with responsibility for budgeting, cash flow, and foreign exchange.

For Susan K. Barnes her NeXT opportunity could be her greatest. She is one of six founders and the chief financial officer of NeXT, the new computer hardware company created by entrepreneurial whiz kid Steven Jobs. Graduating from the Wharton School in financial accounting, Barnes took a job with Arthur Andersen. "I was bored to tears there. The atmosphere was *so* formal." At 27, she became controller at the MacIntosh division of Apple Computer, with responsibility for three plants and a $1 billion budget. When Jobs left Apple, Barnes left too, urging him on to what became NeXT.

Susan King is president of Steuben Glass, the Corning Glass subsidiary respected for its fine design and quality. Highly prized by her CEO and mentor, James Houghton, King was recruited from Washington, D.C., where she served as chairman of the Consumer Product Safety Commission. King is a strong manager with unbounded career ambition. She maintains a 75-hour week and has accepted the challenge of turning around the sometimes innovative, often stodgy Steuben, which faces worldwide competition in the fine glass industry.

A WAVE OF FINANCIAL MANAGERS

Although having a strong marketing track record and a solid mentor relationship are certainly pluses on the path to the top, another of Fraser's stunning findings among the top corporate executives is *their financial acumen and propensity for undertaking rigorous quantitative analysis.* In short, a growing number of CWATTs are good with numbers, big numbers. They understand money and how money works.

Because the corporations have changed and women have moved into tougher, quantitative disciplines, the gates are swinging open. The growing prowess of female corporate executives to manage numbers represents a stark contrast with the earlier stereotype, "Women are not good at finances."

Approximately 30 percent of CWATTs currently hold financial posts with budgets of *$35 million to $18 billion*, and responsibilities for mergers, acquisitions, trade-offs, and top budgetary decisions on international financial transactions. The financial wizards among CWATTs usually started with M.B.A.s in finance, then became management trainees, and progressed to directors of operations and corporate treasurers.

MANAGING BILLIONS IN THE TOUGH OIL INDUSTRY, ETC.

Imagine controlling not just millions, but billions of dollars for one of the world's largest oil refiners.

Camron Cooper

Camron Cooper is treasurer and a senior VP of Atlantic Richfield (ARCO). Her function is typical of other financial experts among CWATTs, however she controls many more dollars, 18,000,000,000 of them.

Cooper was weaned on Wall Street, serving as an analyst and money manager for more than a decade. She was recruited from Wall Street by ARCO, starting in investor relations, and by 1978 she rose to corporate treasurer. Among Cooper's goals is to make a substantial contribution to ARCO's profitability.

Within the past decade she has become a highly respected financial manager within the industry. Her career climb has been carefully calculated with the strong backing of top senior management, including her supportive CEO, Lodwrick Cook. He has watched her succeed in making some of the toughest financial recommendations and decisions, including the downsizing of ARCO as a corporation and the sale of two large subsidiaries.

Nina Dinell

Nina Dinell is treasurer of the Great Atlantic and Pacific Tea Company (A&P). She did not earn her M.B.A. until age 34, though she had been building her career path with the help of several mentors and recruiters. Dinell began her career at the GAF Corporation then moved to the Bank of California.

Dinell is an executive who loves the challenge of high finance. Her financial genius was quickly acknowledged within the food industry; she became assistant treasurer at Supermarkets General, then moved to the post of treasurer for M&M/Mars, where she became the company's first treasurer. Later she was recruited by A&P; they wanted a tough but sensitive financial wizard who could downsize the bumbling giant supermarket chain. "I'm good at fixing things," Dinell says, echoing the sentiments of her colleagues.

Ellen Marram and Ellen Monahan

Ellen Marram is president and chief executive of RJR Nabisco with financial responsibility for the $2 billion biscuit company. Only 43, she is often mentioned as the next woman to become a CEO of a *Fortune 500* company. On the way up, the Harvard M.B.A. achieved major successes in the food division as Oreo and Ritz climbed to record sales. Another Ellen at RJR Nabisco, Ellen Monahan is vice president of corporate planning. Monahan is a 22-year veteran with the corporation helping to form strategy which guides it through challenging times.

Of the many corporations cited for their vigorous efforts in indiscriminately advancing the careers of talented employees, Merck and Company, the progressive $5 billion drug and specialty chemical company, is usually among them. Merck has also been the top vote-getter for several years as "most respected" in *Fortune* magazine's annual poll of major corporate CEOs.

Judy Lewent

Judy Lewent is vice president and treasurer of Merck. With an M.B.A. from M.I.T.'s Sloan School of Business, she set her financial career track into motion with a hitch at E.F. Hutton as an investment banking specialist, moving on to Banker's Trust. A search executive steered her to a controller post at Pfizer. Lewent, respected for her financial acumen, was then recruited by Merck nine years ago, originally as director of acquisitions and capital analysis. As the company continues to expand globally, with the support of mentor Roy Vagelous, the firm's CEO, Lewent has taken on an increasingly larger role in directing the profitable pharmaceutical.

CWATTS IN MARKETING

Corporate marketing is another good path for success. In fact, finance, marketing and human resources are the top three disciplines among CWATTs.

Public relations represents a tougher path to the top. There are some success stories, but as an overall career path, PR does not seem to facilitate the way for upward movement. Within PR there is no apparent career track to top management—it is a staff, not a line position—and salaries tend to top out at $150,000, well under what upper management employees can earn.

Shirley Young

Shirley Young is among a handful of corporate women in top positions coming from a public relations/marketing background. Young is a Wellesley College graduate born in Shanghai. Employed by Gray Advertising in New York, as president of the strategic marketing division, she was a respected "outside" marketing consultant to General Motors. CEO Roger Smith and top management wanted her at GM full time, and when the auto manufacturer ran aground, it sought to hire Young from Gray where she had worked for 30 years. Young is now vice president of Consumer Market Development. GM considers the overachieving Young's contribution to the company critical to its corporate growth.

THE HUMAN RESOURCES ROUTE TO THE TOP

If human relations or human relations development is your forte, you'll be glad to know that human relations management is emerging as a viable route by which to progress to top management. There are rising stars such as in HRD within the insurance industry, travel, computers, apparel, and publishing among other industries with broad responsibility for the implementation of large administration systems, for corporate training programs and for thousands of employees.

RETAILING: AN INDUSTRY IN TRANSITION

Although retail management (at the regional, branch and store level) has been traditionally viewed as a haven for women with managerial skills, retailing at the corporate level hasn't offered women the same kind of stability and clear career progression as other industries. For would-be CWATTs, retailing represents an industry with good potential for *highly creative types*.

Karol D. Emmerich

One of the exceptions is Karol D. Emmerich, who has lasted for 18 years in this rocky industry. Emmerich is vice president and treasurer of the giant diversified retailer, Dayton Hudson, whose revenues exceed $10 billion. She joined Dayton Hudson at age 23, beginning as a financial analyst, then being named assistant treasurer in 1976. Three years later she was offered the treasurer's post.

Linda Wachner

Leading and succeeding in a takeover bid, Linda Wachner is now president and CEO of Warnaco, a major clothing conglomerate. Starting in the cosmetics business, she became president of Max Factor. When the company was sold she fought hard for the opportunity to lead it, then used her financial prowess to succeed in a leveraged takeover bid of Warnaco. She was the first woman to succeed in this manner.

JET SET BUT NOT JET LAG

Women or men at the top must have high energy, the kind that enables them to stay active and in motion for long hours. At the same time, they must be in control of that energy to avoid burnout and excessive stress. CWATTs exhibit well-developed self-discipline and generally are relentless in their career pursuits: nearly all average more than 65-hour work weeks.

Cathleen P. Black is publisher of *USA Today*, owned by the Gannett Company and but one example of many among the Top 50 who is constantly airborne. Occupying this high visibility post, Black, stationed in Washington, D.C., but a frequent passenger on the commuter shuttle to New York, is on the firing line to increase *USA Today*'s advertising revenues.

Particularly among women who work in larger organizations, like their male counterparts, they are jet-setters, often eating breakfast in one country and lunch in another. "Jet set" does not lead to jet lag however, as most are acclimated to this pace and thrive on the excitement and responsibility that goes along with their work.

GOING FIRST CLASS

In airline travel, the first-class compartment has long been a bastion of the old boy network with many executives choosing to travel exclusively in first class because of who else is likely to be seated there. Today, the top female executive is skilled to take maximum advantage of the opportunities that such access provides.

Within the past several years, corporate women at the top (CWATTs) have become masters of the travel "market." Picture this: a woman is sitting in a first-class section on a transatlantic flight. She is dressed in an attractive business suit, is wearing an expensive watch and carrying a serious-looking leather briefcase, and is reading either the *Wall Street Journal*, *Barron's*, *Financial Times of London,* or a stack of company memoranda.

Now the $64,000 question: Will any men in the first-class section *not* be interested in meeting her and finding out just what she does for a living?

Judith H. Monson

Judith H. Monson travels the globe as vice president of finance for Seagram's $2.5 billion international division. She oversees budgets of Seagram affiliates in 28 countries as she develops global strategies, mergers and acquisitions. About the heavy travel schedule she says, "I find it exhilarating, not exhausting. It's a chance to progress in my career and, at the same time, see and learn about the world as few people ever will."

191

Monson, a Harvard M.B.A., joined Seagram as a financial analyst, moving to director of corporate development, then to her current position. Her counterpart at Seagram is Jacque McCurdy, vice president of industry relations. A hard-nosed lawyer, McCurdy began her career in the Maryland state legislature. At Seagram she spends *85 percent of her time on the road* monitoring U.S. legislation and regulation that may impact the industry. She is considered by many as the most powerful woman in the industry.

The Very Friendly Skies

One veteran traveler says, "Traveling first class, I often meet corporate CEOs and search executives, and believe me, after a few minutes they don their recruiter's hat." This executive works 70 hours a week and regularly travels the globe.

"Mobility is part of the territory," she says, "while emotional stamina is crucial. "You can't make it at the top without it. Business is a marathon, not a sprint. People who put a lot of stress into their lives won't make it. You have to maintain a positive outlook."

Among PATTs it can be a small, select world. *Whether in the first-class section of an airplane, the back of a limousine, or in the corporate boardroom, top executives—especially women at the top —circulate within a choice sphere that is to their overwhelming advantage.* In the lofty towers of the corporate boardroom they become highly visible targets for corporate recruiters. CWATTs who excel are hounded by executive search firms who recognize hot commodities when they see them and know firms that compensate them well.

BEING ACCEPTED AS EXECUTIVES

Women in top corporate positions regard themselves simply as executives, not "female" executives. More than a subtle distinction, this is a reflection of personal values. Fraser found that *these women usually do not affiliate with women's groups, feminist causes, or related pursuits.* Many have a distinct distaste for women's issues and organizations. Their main focus and strongest concern? They deeply want to be accepted and respected for their capabilities as executives with "bottom line" talents!

CWATTs, indeed, are singled out within their companies because they are good business leaders, not because they are women. They are constantly striving to prove their business sense and judgment capabilities, and to achieve a string of accomplishments.

> *These women want to be given the ACID test,*
> *walk through fire, run the gauntlet, be put*
> *through the same vigorous paces as the male*
> *executives before them, and continue*
> *to show up as winners.*

Particularly among those that are not married, they're dedication to career can seem overwhelming, even fanatical to an outside observer, and often is. They are driven individuals who want to climb as far up as they can. As a rule, they are on the go. If not married, they will relocate on short notice, and if married, they still are likely to move if it means a more challenging job. In addition, they are loyal to their companies. They usually are on a fast-track and rapidly move up the ranks of their company.

If they are not recognized by their own organizations, however, they may make a job change within their own industries, from one manufacturing concern to another or from one financial institution to another.

ARE FEMALE EXECUTIVES HAPPY?

While high-ranking corporate women experience job pressures as one might expect, they tend to be happy both with their work and themselves. Several yearn for more time for a close personal relationship and some find themselves alone on holidays, but most report being generally pleased about their lifestyles and better adjusted than their pioneer counterparts of 10 to 20 years ago.

In general, corporate women are not as family-oriented as entrepreneurial women. Many cite career commitments as the major contributor to their decision to remain childless. Though the notion persists of "having it all," the corporate women, in particular, find that the demand on their personal time and the travel demands of their jobs have been especially tough.

Those with children use their management planning skills to schedule their work and family time. They often rely on nannies and other support systems to smooth over the rough spots in their lives.

Although deliberate and self-controlled, they tend to be more expressive than the few female executives of the 1970s. Most exercise regularly and fraternize professionally at golf, tennis or the racquet club with other senior executives, and most network extensively at trade association and business meetings.

While they are passionate about their work and the challenges they face, the *younger half* believe they can have it all, including a husband, with the issue of children being a "maybe." The younger half also come equipped with well-developed capabilities to "roll with the punches," and they feel more at ease in the corporate ranks, exhibiting a "you bet I belong" attitude.

In summary, here's the inside word—what Fraser discovered in her extensive study on the behavior of top female corporate executives. Their approach to life and work is as follows.

Be the best you can be. Be tough, resolute and demanding of yourself. Cultivate the passion to succeed; want it in your gut.

Expect diligence and hard work. A 65-hour work week is for real—it is not a figure used just to impress people.

Get an M.B.A. concentrating in finance or marketing and attend continuing management training courses; learn how to number crunch—you cannot escape it on the way up.

Chart and update your direction at work—for what kind of company do you want to work and where? Break out the yellow pads, map the pros and cons.

Read and digest all you can about business in general; subscribe to *Forbes, Fortune, Business Week* and other top business periodicals; continually take in new material and new ideas; and *make your business your career and your hobby*.

Document what you do. Give letter-perfect presentations.

Plan, plan, plan.

Maintain your corporate track record, examine it, and build on it. What else should be included in it?

Find and use mentors on the way up, men and women. Stay friendly with legions of others. Network, affiliate.

Don't make the same mistake twice. Review, learn and keep going forward. Everybody makes mistakes—it's what you do after making them that counts.

Learn and practice diplomacy; it is hard to keep moving up if too many people do not like you.

Move on if your company is holding you back; there are other companies offering positive opportunities. Move in sync with your goals; track and record them.

Put ethics first; things are sure to go better in the long run.

Build a team; your staff can be your strongest asset. Put the human back into human resources.

Instill personal support; and install backup systems to ensure a smooth personal life; i.e., housekeeper, child care, deliveries.

Finally, enjoy the ride and maintain your sense of humor.

Chapter Nine

Hot Tips/Insights

- After years of not being allowed to ascend to top corporate positions, in most major companies female corporate executives today have an open door, with many companies actively grooming their best and brightest. Regardless of a person's gender, in the corporate world the focus is on achieving bottom-line results.

- CWATTs understand money and corporate finance.

- Rising female corporate executives tend be controllers or corporate planners. Many have financial acumen and a propensity for undertaking rigorous quantitative analysis.

- They seek career advancement using the same tools as their forerunners: finding a mentor, offering proven results, networking through business organizations and taking advantage of relationships and contacts made along the way.

- Women at the top in the corporate world are consistent performers—they know that a solid track record is undeniable and required for the journey they've chosen.

- Female corporate executives quietly move forward, they do not flaunt their success with the media as some entrepreneurial types do.

- Most have obtained M.B.A.s.

- Eastern firms generally offer the greatest number of opportunities for aspiring young females executives.

- CWATTs themselves recommend going to a leading business school; joining a progressive company in a line job position; demonstrating results every step of the way;

gaining support from senior male mentors; staying on the upward career track.

- CWATTs dress, speak and present ideas with precision. They take calculated risks. Making their company and their boss look good is of paramount importance.

- One of the smartest moves a rising female star can make is to attract a strong mentor and develop a healthy, long term professional relationship.

- Women or men at the top have high energy, the kind that enables them to stay in motion for long hours, however, they also are in control of that energy so that they avoid frequent burnouts and excessive stress.

- CWATTs generally are relentless in their career pursuits: nearly all average more than 65-hour work weeks.

- Top female executives are skilled to take maximum advantage of the opportunities that flying first class provides such as access to top executives of other organizations.

- CWATTs usually do not affiliate with feminist causes, or related pursuits. Many have a distinct distaste for non-business-related women's issues and organizations.

- They deeply want to be accepted and respected for their capabilities as executives with "bottom line" talents.

- Particularly among those that are not married, they're dedication to career can seem overwhelming, even fanatical to an outside observer, and often is.

Chapter Ten

ENTREPRENEURIAL WOMEN: RISKING FOR REWARD

Opportunities are usually disguised as hard work, so most people don't recognize them.
—Ann Landers

The image, moves, and smarts of successful Entrepreneurial Women At The Top (EWATTs) differs from those of their corporate counterparts. The salient, common characteristic of top entrepreneurial women is their strong ambition to expand their businesses. In fact, women-owned businesses are the fastest-growing segment of the American economy, and the message for women interested in making it to the top of the business world without getting an M.B.A. or doing the corporate shuffle is to start your own business. Depending on one's personality and family situation, this may be the most desirable route.

Women currently own more than 4,000,000 enterprises in the United States, with total revenues exceeding $120 billion, equal to 27 percent of total small business revenues. By the year 2000, female-owned businesses will account for 50 percent of all domestic small businesses and will take in 50 percent of the nation's small-business revenues.

DIVERSE PATHS TO THE TOP

Collectively, entrepreneurial women who have succeeded travel more diverse paths than those of their corporate counterparts. Edie Fraser found that generally, *they gain a wealth of experience prior to age 40*, with the exception of those who took over the business from a husband or parent. Most also have strong people skills—exhibiting the ability to form potent relationships and to inspire others.

More than 80 percent of all small businesses, whether male- or female-headed, start from scratch. Just under 20 percent represent some type of continuation of a family business, whether the entrepreneur inherited the business, worked up the ranks in the company, or had it thrust upon him or her. Business start-ups, among fifty top EWATTs surveyed by Fraser, break down as follows.

Twenty-four came through family liaisons, including twelve who succeeded their husbands and seven who followed their fathers into business.

Twenty-six took the initial plunge alone, without family, including four who bought their businesses; hence, twenty-two founded their companies.

Particularly notable is that *EWATTs do not tend to get M.B.A.s; many do not possess even undergraduate business degrees.* Understandably, they find on-the-job education to be essential.

They quickly recognize the need for financial acumen and either acquire or hire financial management skills.

Many spend several years in business with far less than storybook success. Margie Tingley stepped on land mines on her way to entrepreneurial success. At age 17, she left home to marry a peripatetic Air Force husband. She soon found herself with three small children, a ruptured disk, and then a divorce. With few assets, but with an inherent flair for marketing (and a new husband) she started Tingley Systems, which designs and licenses computer software.

From humble beginnings, Tingley built the business to the $40 million company it is today, providing financial and management software, as well as training. She just completed building a $1 million office facility, while fighting lawsuits on pirating and dealing with hazards of a highly competitive industry. At the same time, as a hobby-business she is designing hand-painted tennis shoes, never tiring in her entrepreneurial pursuits.

MENTORS AND SEERS

To rise to the top in your own venture, *get thee a mentor!* Like the *Fortune 500* executives, EWATTs usually have, or had, a male mentor, sometimes their fathers, possibly a brother or husband. Kay Koplovitz's constant booster is her husband, Bill. She represents one of the few lucky entrepreneurs who started her career in public relations, switching fields to make it to the top in broadcasting.

After serving as public relations director for Communication Satellite Company (COMSAT), then running her own public relations firm, Koplovitz moved into cable television and has made giant strides in just a few short years. She is president and CEO of the USA Network, a leading cable television business. Koplovitz heads one of the more successful privately owned networks, and she has become a highly visible industry executive. She stands up well to strong competition—she has negotiated TV-broadcast rights for major league sports broadcasts, children's cartoon series and leading series like *Murder, She Wrote.*

PROPELLED BY OPPORTUNITY

Whereas female corporate executives use strategic career approaches based on their business school education, successful entrepreneurial women are propelled by perceived opportunity. "The corporate executives plan but do not own their destiny," says Fraser. "The entrepreneurs feel a strong ownership of their destiny." Ownership of her own destiny describes the path of June Collier.

Married at age 16 and mother to two children by age 20, today Collier is chair and CEO of National Industries in Montgomery, Alabama, a manufacturing wiring assembly and antenna business with $120 million in annual revenues. Collier is a high school graduate but did not attend college. She has been committed to her entrepreneurial dream since a young age and has shown the strong persistence needed for her company to grow.

In 1968, Collier bought out one of her partners and brought the company back from bankruptcy. She since has successfully battled considerable competition, both domestic and foreign. She is considered forthright, determined, shrewd, and tough. Her dreams are for her business to carry on into the 21st century through her five children and grandchildren.

WHAT THE CONSUMER WANTS

EWATTs, similar to any successful entrepreneurs, maintain a keen focus on customer wants and needs. In the cosmetics industry, Estee Lauder's dream and driving force was to serve women worldwide. Lauder now retired, her son runs the company today.

Among contemporary cosmetic industry EWATTs, Paula Meehan's strategic start is illuminating. Meehan is the founder of Redken Labs in California, which annually grosses over $115 million. She did not benefit from a formal education or business training; she started in the business world as a model in the late 1950s.

In 1960, using $3,000 of her own money, Meehan conducted her own research to determine how to produce cosmetic products for which she "knew" there would be great demand by consumers. Frustrated by U.S. financial institutions who saw little potential in her products, she eventually raised the capital she needed in Japan from the Bank of Tokyo! By 1971, she successfully took her company public.

Today, Meehan handles the company's overall development efforts, including oversight of the company's legal and governmental activities and expansion into new markets. Her enthusiasm remains to supply women and men worldwide with high-quality products and is reflected in the company's theme: "Dedication to beauty through science."

EXCITEMENT THAT CONVEYS ITSELF TO OTHERS

Entrepreneurial women—just like entrepreneurial men—are excited about business growth and are willing to undertake the risks that lead to growth.

The female entrepreneur is gratified knowing that most of the company's ownership is hers. She maintains a vision of eventually selling out for millions, though she will often mention the desire to keep the business privately owned or within the family.

They thrive on change, and can perceive and capitalize on an opportunity with speed and aplomb. Whereas corporate

203

executives are deliberate, calculating and cautious, EWATTs tend to be freewheeling individuals who keep an eye out for opportunity in whatever form it may disguise itself.

As with some successful EWATTs, Judy Sheppard Missett's business was not planned; it evolved as a passion fueled by her imagination. Missett is synonymous with Jazzercise. The company has approximately 4,000 franchises operating nationwide and is expanding internationally. With her passion, grass-roots marketing sense, love of dancing, and ambition to grow, Missett became the driving force behind this new "movement." She currently is training her daughter to someday take over the Jazzercise business.

THE RAW URGE TO BUILD

When it comes to the number of hours worked per week, entrepreneurial women experience irony. While these entrepreneurs are work horses, often they go into business for themselves for the imagined flexible time. They end up working many more hours than they first conceived.

When EWATTs seize an opportunity, they are willing to pour unlimited energy into making it pay off. They are overly ambitious and glad of this. Fraser observes that they are "endowed with the raw urge to build." Such is the case with Maryles Casto. Her story could be called, "Have Desire, Will Build Travel Agency."

Born and raised in the Philippines, she founded Casto Travel, in 1973. Today she annually grosses over $50 million with plans to greatly exceed that figure. It is the largest privately owned travel agency in northern California, and Casto was cited as the Woman of the Year by the San Francisco Chamber of Commerce.

More than 20 years ago, Casto was enjoying a plush life in her native city of Cebu in the Philippines, where her father was a wealthy sugar and coconut plantation owner. However, her entrepreneurial drive would soon dislodge her from the life of ease.

From an early career with Philippines Airlines, as manager of in-flight service, she came to the United States with an American husband. A female friend, her mentor at the time, and her husband encouraged Casto to work in a travel agency. They bolstered her with inspiring "you can do it" messages. With this vote of confidence, Casto began to learn the travel industry and by 1975, with her friend as partner, she opened Casto Travel on a $1,500 initial investment.

Though pregnant, she began cold-calling—EWATTs in motion are tough to stop. At times she felt a little guilty running a business and being a mother at the same time, since with her family wealth she really did not have to work. However, she knew that she could be both an excellent businesswoman and an excellent mother.

Casto believes that her energy and passion for both business and life keeps her going. "You need to be strong and maintain the initial passion and dedication. It's like a glowing fire in one's belly," she says. "If I lose an account, I lose an account, but I will not make the same mistake," she says. "You only keep building if you seek new answers; keep asking 'why?' Get the right people, give them the support they need, and build, build, build."

Casto Travel now has 140 employees and undoubtedly will surpass the $100 million per-year mark. Casto's quest is to continue to grow. She likes the money, control, and freedom to make decisions; she thrives on risk, innovation, and change. Her advice to future EWATTs: "Reach for the top and don't be afraid. Keep on reaching, and continually work on both your business and personal life. Never think of failure; learn, enjoy the excitement, and maintain the passion."

LACK OF EXPERIENCE IS NO MATCH FOR DESIRE

As many EWATTs have proven, the lack of vast experience is not fatal to succeeding in your own venture. Consider Sybil Ferguson, CEO of Diet Center. As a young woman, she struggled with weight control for 18 years.

In 1968, Ferguson weighed 196 pounds and had tried dozens of diet plans—in those days, however, diets were "in print" only. She was tired of counting calories and the yo-yo-like, up-and-down weight swings that resulted from dieting. Malnutrition became a problem for her as well, and at one point she needed three emergency blood transfusions. Confused and frustrated, she even considered surgery as an alternative to weight loss.

Ferguson went to the local college, read nutrition books and started a plan for herself. It worked. Then she shared it with friends and neighbors—it worked for them too! Ferguson reviewed her program with a physician and then launched the Diet Center with her personal savings. Married with five children, she made it work, though she had no applicable business experience or education. She encouraged her earlier clients to tell others, and the word-of-mouth approach worked very well. The Diet Center grew like wild fire, without advertising.

Before long, she added a proprietary line of vitamins. Ferguson's husband eventually quit his job and joined her. They have since trained thousands of franchise managers including four of her five children. Nineteen grandchildren have also gotten involved in the family business.

"Formal education isn't important. Continuing education and self-learning is, along with personal drive," Ferguson says. She now oversees 2,200 Diet Centers which annually gross more than $200 million in sales. The company has recently gone international with centers opening in Australia, England

and Canada. In the Fall of 1990, the Diet Center helped its 5,000,000th customer to lose weight.

Long hours? "You bet," she exclaims. "It's just a way of life. An entrepreneur is born with a mind that doesn't stop, 18 hours a day. You're driven with a passion and ideas that do not turn off. Even in a social setting you think of new ideas." Ferguson, a Midwestern entrepreneur with traditional values, ranks spirituality first, family second, and business third in importance, but says, "They are all intertwined if you are going to be very successful in business."

"When you're happy and excited about your business," says Ferguson, "your entire life is better. My long-term goal is to continue to help people not just lose weight but makeover their whole lifestyle and make sure it's a better way of life." She is optimistic for future EWATTs, cautioning only that they be sure to make generous time for their families.

FAMILY TIES

As demonstrated by Sybil Ferguson, the family is more important to entrepreneurial women at the top than to corporate women at the top. Fraser's study found that most EWATTs are currently married. Nearly half have children. These numbers exceed marriage and child-rearing statistics among female managers nationally. Even more surprising, and perhaps a key to very long-term success, nearly all have their children in the business!

The entrepreneurs with families express their feelings of inner happiness but feel pressured to meet the numerous demands on their time. Still, they manage to juggle their often competing roles.

Sandra Kurtzig

Sandra Kurtzig, CEO of ASK Computer, established one of the largest entrepreneurial companies in America, annually grossing more than $100 million. Trained in mathematics and engineering, she left General Electric in her late 20s to build ASK, and àt 31, amidst wide publicity, took the company public in 1981.

Though Kurtzig is unflagging in fostering the growth and development of her company, she also relishes the joy of her family. In the rarest of moves—because of her ability to make it work—she stepped down as CEO for a few years to spend time with her children, but then returned to the company in 1989, resuming her leadership position.

Lana Jane Lewis-Brent

In another example of female entrepreneurs interacting with their families is Lana Jane Lewis-Brent president and CEO of Sunshine Stores, a food-retailing chain based in Panama City, Florida. She assumed the presidency of the company after her father died in 1982, and she hopes to have her young son follow her in the business as Sunshine Stores expands across the South.

Marcy Symms and Ellen Gordon

Similarly, Marcy Symms is proud to follow her dad as president of the Symms Corporation, the aggressive New York and Mid-Atlantic discount retail clothing chain. Ellen Gordon also succeeded her father at Tootsie Roll. She brought in her husband, Mel, and has ably guided the company to $200 million in annual revenue, gobbling up Charms Candies in 1988 to add "Dots" to the Tootsie Roll family.

NEITHER DEATH NOR DISRUPTION

Neither divorce, nor quarrels, nor gloom of night keeps the EWATTs from their appointed rounds. *Where there is family con-*

flict or disruption, they continue with the management of their ventures. Their businesses generally weather the challenges and they remain poised for growth.

Enide Allison

Many EWATTs are widows, ably assuming the reins of the company with the passing of their husbands. When Enide Allison's husband died in 1978, she was thrust into the presidency of Allison Motors. Without business experience, she made decisions on "gut" reactions or with the help of her trusted attorney. Soon thereafter she felt compelled to fire her son for the good of the company—a reversal of the norm. She continued building the company and added a second dealership and a parts company. Now 64, Allison runs the highest-grossing Mazda dealership in the United States. Needing additional employees, she decided to rehire her son, and two of her other four children now hold executive positions within the company.

Bea Coleman and Others

In the face of what others might see as serious disruption, the general rule for entrepreneurs is regroup and carry on. Bea Coleman, now in her 70s, is president and CEO of Maidenform, taking over for her husband when he died several years ago. Similarly, following the deaths of their husbands, Helen K. Copley, CEO of Copley Press, and Katharine Graham, matriarch of the *Washington Post*, assumed the corporate leadership for the first time under bereavement.

NOT AFRAID TO FAIL

EWATTs, unlike the corporate executives display raw self-confidence and aggressive action-taking. This enables them to experience serious falls and bounce back unharmed. They know that being down is not being out. They are venturers who understand risk and reward.

> *Many EWATTs have experienced abject failure in earlier ventures. They are able however, to stop, revive themselves, and come back even stronger. Win or lose, they rely primarily on their own resources.*

EWATTs live by a "Who Says I Can't?" credo. When Paula Meehan, cited earlier, was turned down by dozens of domestic banks, she found a way. Mary Kay Ash, grande dame of Mary Kay Cosmetics, began in her garage—with no help—after toiling for years in a company that had no interest in letting her bloom. Lillian Vernon Katz, queen of direct sales with the $150 million dollar-a-year catalogue company bearing her name, began the business on her dining room table. *EWATTs perceive obstacles as challenges, not knock-out punches.*

WOMEN AT THE TOP: A CONTRAST

The chart below contrasts CWATTs and EWATTs as to backgrounds, influences, orientation, and goals.

KEY DIFFERENCES: CORPORATE EXECUTIVES VERSUS ENTREPRENEURS

Corporate Executives	Entrepreneurs
1. *Ambition:* to rise to the top and be recognized as a successful executive	1. *Ambition:* fueled by opportunity and the ability to call their own shots

2.	*Most influenced by:* male mentor or corporate head hunters, company friendships	2.	*Most influenced by:* father or other mentor; i.e., brother, uncle, or mother
3.	*In general:* self-discipline, self-control, deliberateness, and long-term career plan	3.	*In general:* creativity, risk-taking to achieve growth, high energy, and independence
4.	*Orientation to others:* politically astute corporate animal, planned networking, team-building skills	4.	*Orientation to others:* relationships as needed and as they develop, entrepreneurial team
5.	*Strengths, disciplines:* financial acumen, analytical ability, strategic planning, marketing, organizing	5.	*Strengths, disciplines:* on-the-job education, instincts, market focus, flair for building, moves quickly
6.	*Seek:* power, influence, and respect	6.	*Seek:* financial rewards, company growth because "It is mine"
7.	*Work style:* 65+ hours/week, perseverance, patience, build track record, team approach	7.	*Work style:* 70+ hours/week, impatience, leapfrog, opportunity, and market driven
8.	*Control:* exercised by corporate culture, executive peer influence, maintaining proper image	8.	*Control:* self-exercised, the raison d'etre of the entrepreneurial career choice
9.	*Personality:* conformist	9.	*Personality:* open, gregarious

10. *Training:* M.B.A., management courses and seminars, project experience	10. *Training:* on the job, occasional business courses as needed

MORE WOMEN HEADED FOR THE TOP

Women at the top in business are reshaping the demographics of the once male-dominated business world. Harvard demographer David Bloom has forecast that the ascent of corporate women to "high executive levels will be the major development for working women over the next 20 years."

The CWATTs are happy but the EWATTs are happier, freer, and generally enjoy a better family life. Both groups have bright, long-term futures, but the EWATTs, because of their ability to maintain more control over their immediate environment, tend to attain more of what they want sooner. Members of each category like work, challenge, opportunity, travel, and profits. Each is glad to be where she is. Most important, each looks forward to Monday mornings.

Opposite is the composite advice EWATTs have for those who contemplate starting or taking over a venture on the road to the top.

Chapter Ten

Hot Tips/Insights

- Follow your passions, trust your instincts, but get good advice.

- Love your work; it is the only way you'll be able to stay at it 75 hours a week.

- Learn all you can about the business and hire for what you are not good at.

- Produce a business plan; share it with your brain trust, and follow it. Changes are okay, but write them down.

- Set up a board of directors or advisory board early on.

- Balance growth with profitability.

- Leave a little slack time in your schedule for the emergencies in between the emergencies.

- Attend your industry's trade shows and conventions; it is one of the quickest ways of gathering competitor data and formulating new strategy.

- Find an external mentor or two, and listen to him or her.

- Admit when you are wrong; this takes a great burden off of your staff.

- Look for the seeds of opportunity in whatever happens— good or bad developments

- Do not coast; remain on alert even in the best of times.

- Surround yourself with the best possible people; you need every edge you can get.

- Look for little victories whan the big ones are few and far between.

- Make friends with bankers.
- Keep smiling and never give up. NEVER!

PART V

IN MOTION

KEEPING UP WITH THE PACE OF CHANGE

There are two kinds of light—the glow that illuminates, and the glare that obscures.

—James Thurber

Increasingly, people at the top are their own futurists—the changes in society simply come too fast for it to be otherwise. In this closing chapter we'll look at becoming your own futurist, putting common office and communication technology to good use, and a variety of other strategies for staying on top in a rapidly changing world.

Juanell Teague, based in Dallas, is best known as the Business Coach of the Future. She teaches how to custom design your life or business through strategies that transform your professional career and personal life beyond expectation. She's worked with executives from Domino's Pizza, the Zig Ziglar Corporation, the Army and Air Force Exchange Service, and most companies in between.

Teague says: "Anyone can chart his/her professional course to take advantage of current and forthcoming trends and those at the top usually do, or assign the task to a capable assistant. Foreknowledge of important business and social trends provides a competitive edge in any field." Teague says becoming your own futurist frees you from the many uncertainties of tomorrow by being several steps ahead today.

"Experts say the world has changed more in the last 45 years than it did in the preceding 4,500," observes Teague. "The first half of the 1990s will bring more change than in all of the preceding 4,545 years. Reaction time is now reduced to nothing."

Predicting future trends often is a crucial capability of those at the top of their professions who wish to remain there. This is especially true for entrepreneurs because customers expect them to know more than they do, to be way ahead of the competition, mapping new terrain, but it is also true for senior executives who face shifting markets and global competition.

PATTs know that ignoring trends is risky. Many organizations begin to decline because too much energy is spent solving immediate problems with no time left over to calculate and plan for the future. As things change, PATTS learn to anticipate that change and remain a few steps ahead.

PREDICTING FUTURE TRENDS

Teague advises reading the right books. She believes that John Naisbitt's *Megatrends* and Naisbitt and Aburdene's *Megatrends 2000* are the classics in the field. "Read them thoughtfully and decide where they hit the mark, where they missed the mark and how you have been affected by the changes discussed," she advises. One of the megatrends Naisbitt pinpointed in 1982 was the explosion of small business starts. The self-help trend also added a new dimension to entrepreneurism.

Teague's Other Recommendations

Read *Strategies 2000* by Carolyn Corbin and Knight Kiplinger's *The New American Boom: Changes in American Life and Business.*

Subscribe to publications such as John Naisbitt's biweekly *Trend Letter.* This is one of the best ways to keep current. One day a client from Detroit was sitting in Teague's office. As they discussed his declining business as a retail consultant, she pulled the latest *Trend Letter* out of her files. The lead story described how the trend toward superstores and small boutiques was squeezing out the medium-sized market. Based on this information, the client decided to restructure his marketing plan and focus his solicitations on small retail environments. Immediately he noted a marked increase in sales.

The *Kiplinger Texas Letter*, a biweekly publication, and the *Kiplinger Washington Letter*, a weekly newsletter, are also excellent ways to learn about local trends while they are still in their early stages. Kiplinger also publishes monthly California and Florida letters.

The New York Times and the *Wall Street Journal* are always sure bets to keep you current. *Entrepreneur* and *Success* are both good magazines to read regularly. In addition, you should subscribe to magazines and professional journals in your own particular field of interest.

Publishers Weekly lists the leading books currently for sale and tells what is coming out onto the market in the next season, and hence tips you off as to what the mass market will be reading and concerned about in the near future.

You can also join the World Future Society, an international association dedicated to working for a better future. As a member you will receive their magazine, *The Futurist*, along with various other helpful publications that deal with future trends.

The newspaper is another important indicator of trends. Newspapers attempt to select news topics on the basis of greatest interest to readers. If last month the paper carried ten articles on female weight lifters and this month it carried 15, you can be sure the interest in women's weight training is probably on the rise.

Keep track of what is going on by watching news shows like *20/20, 60 Minutes, West 57th Street,* etc. Learn about social issues by watching *Donahue* and/or the *Oprah Winfrey Show.*

Become familiar with the leading financial indicators—sales of real estate and cars, the state of the oil industry, trends in the stock market and international finance.

Teague recommends increasing your powers of observation by always asking yourself: What is going to be the likely result of this particular event? How will this influence the trends for the future?

"If you can discover what people's needs and desires are going to be in the future, you can prepare yourself ahead of time and prosper by meeting those needs," says Teague. "With a little determination and some knowledge of where to look and what to look for, you can learn to predict the future." This will give you the edge and better positioning required for sustained success.

PUTTING TECHNOLOGY TO GOOD USE

The word "technology" can mean everything from lasers to robots to space stations. Office and communication technology afford PATTs instant information when they need it. They now have the ability to be in touch with their offices—remaining productive, wherever they are—and they can set up an environment that eases workloads and even stimulates creativity.

On a corporate scale, the rise of Federal Express came in large part from its investment in new tools—computer technology to track accurately the packages it sends around the world every night. Meanwhile, industry leader UPS was content with its largely manually based system. Only after it lost a large part of its market share did it throw its capital reserves into a billion-dollar effort to modernize traffic management.

On an individual level, the well-equipped office can be fun as well as supportive. The chairman of one company is proud to show off his desk command post complete with an intercom phone to summon subordinates, and a combination of scissors, stapler, tape dispenser and hole punch. He also totes a credit card-sized calculator wherever he goes. "Indispensable on the job," he says.

The key to using business tools is being selective.
PATTs don't tend to get swept up in the newest toys
and they don't lose sight of why they are purchasing
a state-of-the-art work-saving device.

PERSONAL COMPUTERS, FINALLY FOR EVERYONE

By far the most pervasive tool of success in the last ten years has been the personal computer. A study on management in the 1990s by the Massachusetts Institute of Technology and the consulting firm of Ernst & Young found, to nobody's great surprise, that senior level managers can no longer afford to be ignorant of information vital to their work efforts and the technology which can make it more readily available.

Before Apple Computer and IBM brought computers to millions of desktops, computer technology was the province of the trained priesthood of managers of information system: MIS. Now, decision makers on all levels have the power to accomplish their own tasks without relying on technocrats.

While using a computer may be second nature to those who grew up with computers in the last decade, for many veteran professionals, as well those re-entering the work force, a computer is daunting. "Isn't it easier just to do things the way I always have?" The answer is probably no. If it involves information, it's likely you can't avoid using a computer to get and store information efficiently.

Increasingly, effectively using available technology will separate PATTs from would-be PATTs. Futurist and corporate consultant Dan Burrus speaks of the many senior executives he encounters both in corporations and other organizations who claim that they have no need to work with their own PC or to learn new programs because they have staff who "take care of that."

Burrus suggests that this line of reasoning is lame and detrimental to their careers. He recommends having staff members continue to handle the routine on their PCs, while the top executive uses *his PC* for other things that no one else can do, such as long-term planning, projections, and "What if?" types of analyses.

At 1600 Pennsylvania Avenue

Having information available when they want it makes personal computers so attractive to PATTs. At 1600 Pennsylvania Avenue, one need look no further down the chain of command than White House Chief of Staff, John Sununu to find a computer devotee. Sununu doesn't delegate his information to deputies. He's ordered his own high-powered desktop computer to run budget calculations and write memos on his own, just as he did while serving as New Hampshire's governor before joining the Bush administration in 1989. Sununu likes the hands-on, instant analysis that he is able to get by working directly with his own computer on his own desk.

Another computer power tool that has found its way into the executive suite is project management software. In fact, business schools, including the prestigious Kellogg Graduate School of Management at Northwestern University in Chicago, now include computerized project management in their curriculum. Project management programs enable one to enter project data and compare it with available resources.

Once the vital data is entered, project management software then facilitates mapping out a time-line or Gantt chart. The program automatically handles resources or schedule changes. Advanced packages go further, drawing time-lines with critical paths—the tasks that have to be completed to keep the project on track.

In the basic microcomputer market, there are two "families" of systems. One family is centered around IBM's line of personal computers, first released in 1981. The other major microcomputer player has been Apple Computer. Its Macintosh family of computers, first introduced in 1984, brought an unprecedented simplicity to computing and also spawned a change in how documents are produced.

While the two camps—IBM and MacIntosh—both have loyal, sometimes fanatic adherents, many of the real differences are disappearing: new Macintosh units have speed and power specifications approaching and sometimes exceeding PCs; IBM, meanwhile, plans to introduce a "point and shoot" Macintosh-like capability for its high-end microcomputers and accompanying software is already being sold by third-party software companies for existing PC computers.

YOU *CAN* TAKE IT WITH YOU

Traditionally, once one left his office, he left bigger tools, including desktop computers, behind. Many PATTs, however, always have something else to do, and they have taken to the latest line of portable laptop computers in droves. While there was initial concern by the airlines and Federal Aviation Administration, laptops have become ubiquitous on cross-country flights. The only caveat to using one is that you will be expected to show the guards that you really are toting a computer, by turning it on at the x-ray security station. This means that you need to be sure that your batteries are fully charged.

True laptops are in the IBM camp, not Apple, and are briefcase-sized, weighing twelve pounds or less. For those at the top, juggling several projects at once, being able to send or get computer data on the run, has proven to be a godsend. It's like having your own telex system—except you can send spreadsheets and other information, not just text messages.

Journalists, who use laptops to file their stories on deadline, know various mildly illegal means of jerry-rigging telephone equipment to send in their stories. Fortunately, most business hotels in the United States and much of Europe are now equipped to allow laptop-to-phone-line connections without technical heroics. Even if a room isn't directly wired for a laptop, most hotel maintenance services can add an extra jack for a fee.

To use a laptop as a communications device, it must be equipped with a modem, which translates data into signals that can be sent on phone lines. Modems come in different speeds. Besides sending information to the office, a laptop computer with a modem can tap into a plethora of services—wire service headlines, industry-specific news, even stock and commodity quotes.

Some networks allow one to open an electronic mail account for sending and receiving electronic memos from other network users. A few services, such as MCI Mail, enable one to send electronic memos to fax machines, but the fax service usually doesn't work in reverse.

A common scenario for many an executive is as follows: catch an early morning flight, fire up the laptop computer to polish a speech to be delivered later to stockholders, or to work through a new set of financial projections, or to complete the monthly memo for the field staff. Upon arriving, he has the new speech text, or financial projections, printed out on a desktop computer system with printer.

After the speech, he can connect his laptop computer to the phone line and touch base with the office—looking for computer messages and getting an electronic report with the month's sales statistics that he reviews on his afternoon flight.

He makes another quick call to an information service to see if his speech had any effect on the price of his company's stock. Then it's off to the airport and another working flight.

Lighter, Faster

The more omnipresent laptops become, the less senior executives are willing to type with, let alone even carry, a relatively light one. As we saw in Chapter One, the power playing CEO doesn't even carry a briefcase. Many PATTs prefer microcassette tape recorders to take down their thoughts as fast as they can say them. With voice activation and auto-reverse to automatically change direction at the end of a side, one only needs to keep a fresh set of batteries and a spare tape—a single 60-minutes-per-side microcassette can easily hold material equivalent to 80 double-spaced pages.

STAYING ORGANIZED

While electronic office technology sends communications at the speed of light, paper-and-pencil methods still have a place in organizing for success. Large appointment books may look like props of the over-organized, but for those with busy work and leisure schedules who need mobility and direct access to information, there are still few real alternatives.

A simple calendar may work for some, but PATTs have too complicated a work and leisure schedule to track just appointments. They need to have phone and fax numbers with them, project notes, and other data. An organizer is unbeatable for providing information in one source that is portable and doesn't require the space or start-up time of a laptop computer. Old standbys, the Filofax and Day-Timer have been joined by a plethora of other organizer systems sold via retail outlets.

You can choose the forms you want to match the way you work. You'll find yourself asking questions: Do I think chronologically or should I break projects down by subject? Do I need to keep a log of calls I make to people? Do I want a lot of space to record a day's events in detail, recording activity for every five minutes? Or do I want a simple daily calendar sheet? Through long years of trial and error many PATTs have devised their own organizer system.

Paper organizers have been issued in electronic form—about the same size as the books they try to replace. Unlike laptop computers, electronic organizers have hard-wired programs and can't run commercial software programs. Electronic organizers—such as the Sharp Wizard and the Casio Boss—include programs to hold schedules, addresses and even write simple memos, which can be loaded onto a full-fledged computer when you return to the office. These are usually the size of a 5-by-8-inch index card, and can fit in a suit pocket. More rudimentary office technology—the size of credit cards—store phone numbers and also work as calculators.

TELECOMMUNICATIONS

Pacific Telesis credited the exploding cellular phone market as a major cause for its decision to add a third area code in grid-locked Los Angeles County. While car phones are no longer a status symbol they have taken hold as a vital tool for success on the road.

One devotee is the owner of several manufacturing companies and a chain of weekly suburban newspapers along Chicago's North Shore. He was skeptical when he first received a cellular phone. Balancing his manufacturing business with his growing chain of newspapers, however, he quickly found his car phone indispensable. Able to talk with customers and employees while on the go has nearly doubled his productive work day, leaving him more time at home and to work on his weekly editorials.

Completely portable phones—not to be confused with cordless phones that are tied to their range from a cradle—are starting to take hold. Motorola is offering a portable cellular phone so compact, it can fit in a shirt pocket. The phone's mouth speaker flips outward, revealing the touch-tone keypad, à la Star Trek.

FAX WITH FLAIR

Everybody has a fax machine in the office; what makes this tool crucial to success is how you use it. An executive at a small computer integration firm in Washington, D.C., routinely uses a fax machine to file legal complaints against federal contract actions that harm his company. Stephen Mills, a vice president at Federal Systems Group Inc., sent a protest brief to the General Services Board of Contract Appeals. At the same time, he sent a copy to a government agency whose solicitation for computers, he claimed, illegally locked his company out of the bidding.

Because the protest would prevent the agency from continuing with its purchase, Mills quickly got a call from the government, and was able to gain approval on a simple change in the requirements that would let him bid on the contract. Before noon—roughly three hours after first filing his complaint—he faxed a dismissal request to GSA, closing the case. While there isn't a Guinness Book of Federal Contracting Records, the Federal Systems Group case is probably the most quickly resolved case and among the most effective three hours anyone has spent in dealing with the Federal government, thanks to the clever use of standard technology.

Fax transmissions have also been used to file for political primaries, make large purchases, announce price changes and simply stay in touch.

The proliferation of fax machines also has brought about the phenomenon of junk faxes. In fact, lists of fax numbers are selling at premium prices to lists of telephone numbers and addresses. The less widely known your fax number is, the less likely you are to become a junk fax target. Some executives have two fax machines—a "public" machine whose number is freely given and a "private" machine used only for outgoing messages or available only to a limited number of outsiders.

OFFICE ENVIRONMENTS

Designing your own highly efficient work environment is another important way to achieve the competitive advantage.

PATTs often make a strong first impression on visitors to their office, but that first impression isn't necessarily awe.

With corporate America becoming leaner, large offices for top management are being viewed as unseemly. Smaller, less formal, more inviting offices are becoming more common. The well-designed, highly functional office today can run from $200 per square foot up to a staggering $500 per square foot.

The quest isn't to create a showplace as much as a very efficient, livable workspace. For example, Donald Carter, chairman of the Carter Organization, which was involved in more than half of U.S. corporate takeovers in the late 1980s, reputedly had a security system designed to accommodate his live-in cat. Carter also installed a private gymnasium and a murphy bed for very late nights at work. Another executive created an office that functioned as a second home. His desk and computer are on the upper level, while below is a sunken living room, complete with a fireplace.

You spend most of your working hours at your desk—so make sure it is set up as efficiently as possible. One of the best ways to display a sense of style while remaining comfortable at one's desk is to have an attractively designed work space. Desks can be made of wood, such as a pine slab supported by an oak pedestal, or stone, such as a slate, granite, or marble for the surface, or even glass. PATTs invariably face their desks outward; facing a wall indicates one who is subservient to others. Besides, as anyone who has been in a position of power will tell you, speaking over your own desk creates a subconscious power balance in your favor.

PATTs are particular about their seats, and with good reason. A long day (and night) of work requires a chair that does not leave you cramped, sore, or tired. A comfortable chair helps to keep you going when you are fatigued and provides appropriate support for your back. Height is important for keeping arms at a comfortable level and preventing muscle fatigue. With a chair that is too low, you feel as if you have been lifting weights for hours on end. The chair back should allow you to change position to shift the muscles used to sit up.

CONDITIONING YOUR ENVIRONMENTS

There are different schools of thought about how to organize a desk. Some argue that a clean desk is the sign of a clear and organized mind, among them, Joseph Sugarman, the previously cited president of a successful direct mail supply company.

Sugarman, who writes those JS&A direct mail ads appearing in the airline magazines, absolutely insists that all of his employees clear their desks every night no matter what they're working on. It's a little extra work but it automatically ensures that the next day only the most important work will be pulled out again, and it's amazing to see what happens by following this simple principle.

It's a truism today: Life is a desk. To prehistoric man, life was a spear and fire. To the frontiersman, life was a rifle. Today life is a desk. One's desk should be a comfortable place—it has to be. The quality and ambience of your work space must demonstrate the quality and ambience of your life or how you would like your life to be.

GGGGGGGGGGGGGGGGGGGGGGGGGGGGGGGGGGGG

THE 10 COMMANDMENTS OF DESKMANSHIP

1. Thou shalt Clear thy desk every night—Yes, every night

2. Thou shalt continuously Refine what goes on thy desk top

3. Thou shalt Not use thy desk top as a filing cabinet

4. Thou shalt predetermine what belongs Inside thy desk

5. Thou shalt keep at least 20 percent of thy drawer space Vacant

6. Thou shalt Furnish thy surrounding office to support thy desk

7. Thou shalt take Comfort when at thy desk

8. Thou shalt keep Clean thy desk and thy surrounding area

9. Thou shalt Leave thy desk periodically

10. Thou shalt Honor thy desk as thyself

Jeff Davidson © 1990

GGGGGGGGGGGGGGGGGGGGGGGGGGGGGGGGGGG

Beyond arranging your office space is the larger notion of controlling your environments. In a rapidly changing world, to effectively set up your office environment (and home, car, and other environments as well) in accordance with what one faces today, is to accommodate inefficiency. To manage time effectively now and in the future, Stanley M. Davis, Ph.D., says that we must learn to manage the beforehand—the beforehand, as opposed to the aftermath.

What is managing the beforehand? Managing the beforehand involves creating space—mentally or physically—in advance of what comes next. It requires anticipation, forethought, and vision. It is an approach for integrating your life's activities with how you decide to keep your office and desk, closets, car and other spaces. It is undertaken by clearing out the old and unsupportive, and making room for *what's next* because in the life of someone headed for the top the best is yet to come.

IN CONCLUSION

As we have seen and discussed throughout this book, the people who make it to the top of their respective professions are different from the rest. They take the time and effort to continually examine the path they've charted and then steadfastly work at implementing effective strategies for business and social success. They learn what it takes to project the right image and make the right moves to climb to the peak in their fields, knowing that enjoying the journey is as important as arriving at the chosen destination.

Chapter Eleven

Hot Tips/Insights

- Increasingly, because of today's rapid changes in business and society, PATTs are their own futurists.

- Predicting the future is crucial for entrepreneurs because customers expect them to know more than they do, but it also true for executives who face shifting markets and global competition.

- To keep up on major and significant trends one needs to regularly read several key magazines and newsletters, such as those listed starting on page 219.

- Practice increasing your powers of observation. Ask yourself: What is going to be the likely result of this particular event? What does this indicate about future trends?

- Finding your own work tools and creating your own work space is a form of undercover work, and a vital way to achieve a competitive advantage.

- Increasingly, effectively using available technology will separate PATTs from would-be PATTs.

- PATTs have taken to the latest line of portable computers in droves.

- Many PATTs prefer microcassette tape recorders, with voice activation and auto-reverse in order to automatically change direction at the end of a side, to take down their thoughts.

- Large appointment books are still popular for those with busy work and leisure schedules who need mobility and direct access to information.

- While car phones are not a status symbol they have taken hold as a vital tool for success.

- PATTs make a strong first impression on visitors to their offices with smaller, less formal, more inviting offices, which are becoming more common.

- There are different schools of thought about how to organize a desk. The prevailing wisdom is that a clean desk is the sign of a clear and organized mind.

- One's desk should be a comfortable place. The quality and ambience of your work space must demonstrate the quality and ambience of your life or how you would like your life to be.

- Enjoying the journey to the top is as important as arriving at the chosen destination.

BIBLIOGRAPHY

BOOKS

Baldrige, Letitia. *Letitia Baldrige's Complete Guide to Executive Manners*. New York: Rawson, 1985.

Beveridge, Don, Jr., and Jeffrey Davidson. *The Achievement Challenge: How to Be a "10" in Business*. Homewood, IL: BusinessOne-Irwin, 1987.

Carnegie, Dale. *How to Win Friends and Influence People*. New York: Simon & Schuster, 1936.

Cialdini, Robert, Ph.D. *Influence: The New Psychology of Modern Persuasion*. New York: Morrow, 1985.

Cohen, Herb. *You Can Negotiate Anything*. New York: Lyle Stuart, 1981.

Davidson, Jeffrey. *Avoiding the Pitfalls of Starting Your Own Business*. New York: Shapolsky, 1990.

Davidson, Jeffrey. *Blow Your Own Horn*. New York: AMACOM Books, 1987.

Dawson, Roger. *You Can Get Anything You Want*. New York: Simon & Schuster, 1985.

Elsea, Janet, Ph.D. *First Impression, Best Impression*. New York: Simon & Schuster, 1986.

Fisher, Roger, Ph.D., and William Ury, Ph.D. *Getting to Yes*. New York: Penguin, 1983.

Garfield, Dr. Charles. *Peak Performance*. New York: Morrow, 1986.

Givens, Charles. *Creating Wealth*. New York: Simon & Schuster, 1986.

Gschwandtner, Gerhard. *Superachievers*. Englewood Cliffs, NJ: Prentice-Hall, 1984.

Gunther, Max. *The Luck Factor*. New York: Ballantine, 1978.

Harris, Louis. *Inside America*. New York: Vintage, 1987.

Korda, Michael. *Power*. New York: Ballantine, 1975.

Martin, Judith. *Miss Manners' Guide to the Turn of the Millennium*. New York: Ballantine, 1989.

McCormack, Mark. *What They Don't Teach You at Harvard Business School*. New York: Bantam, 1984.

Mrkvicka, Edward. *Bank Book: Revoking Your Bank's License to Steal*. New York: Perennial Library, 1989.

Naisbitt, John, and Patricia Aburdene. *Mega-Trends 2000*. New York: Morrow, 1990.

Pelton, Warren, et al. *Tough Choices*. Homewood, IL: BusinessOne-Irwin, 1989.

RoAne, Susan. *How to Work a Room*. New York: Shapolsky, 1988.

Robbins, Anthony. *Unlimited Power*. New York: Simon & Schuster, 1986.

Scheele, Dr. Adele. *Skills for Success*. New York: Ballantine, 1987.

Sugarman, Joseph. *Success Forces*. Chicago: Contemporary Books, 1980.

Toffler, Alvin. *The Third Wave*. New York: Morrow, 1980.

ARTICLES

"Achievement Motive," by David McClelland, Ph.D., in *Harvard Business Review*, December 1965.

"Astute PR transforms Ollie North's Image," by Jonathan Blum, in *Marketing News*, September 11, 1987.

"Banks Need Depositers," by Augustin Hedburg, in *Money*, March 1988.

"Behavior Patterning," by Gerry Tausch, in *The Meeting Manager*, October 1985.

"Boss Offices," by Sally Robbins, in *Psychology Today*, October 23, 1989.

"Boy Scout Billionaire," by David Remnick, in *Town & Country*, October 1987.

"Breaking Up Is Complex to Do," by Eric Schmuckler, in *Forbes*, October 24, 1988.

"CEOs See Clout Shifting," by Thomas Stewart, in *Fortune*, November 6, 1989.

"Communicate Your Way to Success," by Adena Givens, in *Charles Givens' Financial Digest*, April 1990.

"Dutiful Wife Hires Husband," by Laura Litvan, in *Washington Times*, June 26, 1990.

"Eagle Scout with a Bloody Nose," by Gerhard Gschwandtner, in *Personal Selling Power*, July/August 1990.

"George Wells: People Power in Plaid," by Valerie Rice, in *Electronic Business*, January 9, 1989.

"How to Influence with Integrity," Laura Gschwandtner, in *Personal Selling Power*, January/February 1990.

"How to Live with a Billionaire," by Alan Farnham, in *Fortune*, September 11, 1989.

"It's What You Do—Not When You Do It," a United Technologies advertisement.

"Keeping It in the Family," by Richard Kirkland, Jr., in *Current*, January 1987.

"Once You've Arrived, Why Wait in Line?" by Sara Bartlett, in *Business Week*, April 27, 1987.

"Q & A on Banking," interview with Edward Mrkvicka, in *Money*, June 1989.

"Rebirth of a Salesman," by Don Oldenberg, in *Washington Post*, February 17, 1987.

"The World's Richest Man," by Patrick Sabatier, in *World Press Review*, November 1987.

"What Good Are B-Schools?" by Robert Samuelson, in *Newsweek*, May 14, 1990.

SPECIAL REPORTS

"The Landmark MIT Study: Management in the 1990s," a five-year MIT research program sponsored by Ernst & Young, 1990.

"Success in America: The CIGNA Study of the Upper Affluent," a Louis Harris and Associates report, commmisioned by CIGNA Individual Financial Services Company, February 1987.

INDEX

INDEX